KEIGHLEY & WORTH VALLEY
LOCOMOTIVES

Tom Heavyside

Midland Publishing Limited

Published in England by
Midland Publishing Limited
24 The Hollow, Earl Shilton, Leicester, LE9 7NA
Tel: 01455 847815, Fax: 01455 841805

© 1996, Tom Heavyside and
Midland Publishing Limited

ISBN 1 85780 050 8

Printed in England by Clearpoint Colourprint Limited
Salop Street, Daybrook, Nottingham, NG5 6HD

Designed by Midland Publishing and
Stephen Thompson Associates

Front cover: **While shedded at Carnforth in the mid-1960s, Stanier 'Black 5' 4-6-0 No 45212 provides a fine spectacle at Thrimby Grange, between Penrith and Shap, on the West Coast main line.** Colour-Rail

Title page: **In July 1960 the driver of the down 'Golden Arrow' walks forward to check that everything is in order at the front end of 'West Country' Pacific No 34092 *City of Wells*, shortly before the train is due to depart from London's Victoria station.**
Don Cash

Back cover, top: **Ex-GWR 0-6-0PT No 5775 is seen at Old Oak Common shed in London on 23rd June 1963, during the course of its transfer from BR to its new owners, London Transport. It was withdrawn from Pontypool Road shed in January of that year.** Colour-Rail

Back cover, bottom: **Waggon & Maschinenbau 4-wheeled diesel railbus No E79962 waits at Audley End, Essex, in 1962.**
B Henderson collection / Colour-Rail

Below: **The coaling of locomotives at the NCB Philadelphia depot, County Durham, was reminiscent of the method employed at some BR sheds. Full wagons were propelled onto the gantry and the coal fed by chutes into the waiting bunkers below. There were few industrial locations which could justify facilities such as this, coal usually having to be shovelled by hand into the bunkers – a time consuming and somewhat laborious task. Here, NCB No 52, the former Taff Vale Railway 0-6-2T No 85, along with NCB No 8, a Robert Stephenson & Hawthorns 0-6-0ST (works No 7691 of 1952), wait patiently by the coaling stage in 1967. No 52 no longer carries a former GWR style safety-valve bonnet, as seen on page 70. No 52 moved to the Keighley & Worth Valley Railway in 1970.**
Ivo Peters

ACKNOWLEDGEMENTS

First, I must place on record my grateful thanks to all the photographers who trawled through their collections at my request, in search of suitable material. Photographs used are credited individually, but equal thanks are due to those whose pictures were unable to be included, due to space constraints, for often snippets of information on the back of prints have helped to complete the history of an engine's past.

Help has been received from many sources, far too numerous to mention individually, including, not least, past owners of some of the stock. Individuals and firms have searched their old records in response to my queries, in the quest to present as complete a record as possible.

Undoubtedly the biggest vote of thanks should be reserved for that fine body of people – the members of the Keighley & Worth Valley Railway Preservation Society, who in the 1960s fought hard to make sure that a pair of parallel rails was retained in operable condition along the floor of the Worth Valley. Since then, they have ensured that the railway has gone from strength to strength. Without the combined efforts of scores of like-minded individuals, this volume in the 'As They Were' series would not have been possible. Thank you all.

Tom Heavyside
Bolton   April 1996

A varied line-up of motive power outside the four-road Leamington Spa shed (then 84D) on 8th July 1962, as future Worth Valley locomotive No 41241 keeps company with home-based Collett 2-6-2T No 4176, and Stanier 8F 2-8-0 No 48264 from Nuneaton (2B). On the right is diesel-shunter No D3974 (later No 08806) from Tyseley (84E). Later, the Ivatt was to be allocated to Leamington, for six months, from January 1964. Ron Herbert

INTRODUCTION

The Keighley & Worth Valley Railway has established itself as one of the foremost preserved railways in the United Kingdom, and a leading tourist attraction in West Yorkshire. Today, it is as much an integral part of the culture of Haworth and the Worth Valley, as is the Bronte family. Within walking distance of Haworth station, albeit by a rather steep climb, is the old parsonage where the famous literary Bronte sisters, Emily of *Wuthering Heights* fame, Charlotte author of *Jane Eyre*, and the lesser known Anne who wrote *Agnes Grey*, lived with their father, the Reverend Patrick Bronte in the mid-nineteenth century.

The first railway to arrive in Keighley was the Leeds & Bradford Railway extension line from Shipley, in 1847. The L&B was soon absorbed by the Midland Railway, but it was another 20 years, on 13th April 1867, before any rails along the Worth Valley were open to the public. In fact, this only came about after much lobbying by local merchants, who in the end, with the backing of the Midland, had to promote the line themselves.

The pioneer Keighley & Worth Valley Company, operated by the Midland, remained in existence until 1886, although the Derby-based moguls had taken full control of day-to-day running from 1881. The branch passed to the London Midland & Scottish Railway at the Grouping in 1923 and, of course, became vested in the state from 1st January 1948.

For nigh on 100 years, the five-mile branch was a valued method of communication for the traders and residents of the Valley, set amidst some harsh and difficult terrain, and where road travel has never been easy. However, under the prevailing economic climate of the late 1950s, the branch service could not be allowed to continue unhindered.

In July 1959 BR issued a notice of closure in respect of the branch passenger service. By dint of some effective local opposition a quick execution was staved off – but not for long, for despite operating an improved diesel service from June 1960, BR were still desirous of deleting Ingrow West, Oakworth, Haworth and Oxenhope from its timetables. Damems, the other station on the line, had been closed in 1949. The last BR public passenger trains passed through the Worth Valley on 30th December 1961. Goods facilities were maintained for another six months.

However, as the curtain came down on BR operations, the events of the mid-nineteenth century were set to repeat themselves. A few determined locals, notably Ralph Povey, the current President of the Keighley & Worth Valley Railway Preservation Society, and the late Bob Cryer, later to become a well-respected Member of Parliament, were set to commence a vigorous campaign for the restoration of services. This time it was not just the locals, for they were soon joined by many other equally resilient people, from far and wide, who shared the same objectives.

After a couple of meetings in early 1962, the Keighley & Worth Valley Railway Preservation Society was founded. There then ensued, six long and often frustrating years of negotiations, fund raising and lobbying, before, at long last, the reopening special was able to clamber noisily out of Keighley, to much acclaim, on 29th June 1968, and mark the start of a new epoch.

Locomotives and stock started to arrive at Haworth, the administrative and operating centre of the line, from 1965. The first was ex-Lancashire & Yorkshire Railway 0-4-0ST No 51218, in January of that year. Since then a veritable wealth of rolling stock, both steam and diesel, has been based on, or has visited, the line.

Lostock Hall shed, Preston, on 3rd August 1968. Stanier class 5 4-6-0s Nos 45305 and 45212 stand side by side as they await their last duties in BR ownership. That day few could have foreseen that both engines would escape the clutches of the scrap-metal dealers, let alone for a time during the early 1990s, that they would again line-up on adjacent tracks on the privately owned Keighley & Worth Valley Railway. No 45305 has since moved on to pastures new.
David Idle

This volume concentrates, in words and pictures, on the diverse history of the locomotives which regard the Keighley & Worth Valley Railway as their normal base, including those of the Bahamas Locomotive Society, who opted to move lock, stock and barrel, to the line, after considering a number of options, following their enforced vacation of the Dinting Railway Centre, near Glossop, in 1990.

Individually, every locomotive on the line, has a deserved and valued place in the preserved railway world. Collectively, they form a treasure trove of immense historical value, the majority of which are intended to operate at some time or other, in the main, hauling tourists simply intent on having a good day out, but also providing a service for the inhabitants of the Valley, who oft-times find the railway the best way of travelling to Keighley.

The diversity of the steam stock can be gleaned quickly from a few facts. In size and power they range from small, humble 0-4-0ST shunting locomotives, to a main line Pacific and three mighty 2-8-0 freight engines. Seven were built during the nineteenth century, the oldest *Bellerophon* in 1874, while there are four comparative youngsters from the 1950s. Represented amongst previous owners are all four BR constituent companies, and four from the pre-Grouping era, alongside a wide variety of industrial users. They are the products of six main line company workshops, and 12 private locomotive builders, two of which are American.

The steam stud is complemented by a not as extensive, but equally diverse, collection of diesel motive power. The KWVR has never been a body to shun these, realising from the very early days their usefulness for off-peak services,

or for a commuter orientated timetable, should this ever get off the ground. Also, they are valued for works and shunting movements.

The KWVR has the use of four diesel locomotives originally owned by BR – two shunters and two Type 2s. Another four shunters have been obtained from industrial locations, while *Vulcan* is an experimental locomotive from 1956, which spent three years on loan to BR. In addition there are two diesel railbuses and a class 108 two-car diesel multiple unit.

On a normal operating day, the visitor to the KWVR will find one or two locomotives in steam. During a gala event there may be up to seven or eight. When not in service the engines can usually be found in Haworth yard, or at either of the museum complexes, situated by Ingrow and Oxenhope stations. It should be remembered, that at any given time, a number of the engines may be in a state of dismemberment, while being overhauled. On occasions, some could be away for short periods on loan to other preserved railways, or hauling main line specials. Conversely, engines based elsewhere can sometimes be found at the head of KWVR trains.

In the pages that follow, the locomotives which became part of BR's fleet are dealt with in a numerical sequence dictated by their British Railways numbers beginning with pannier tank No 5775 and ending with standard class 4 2-6-4 tank No 80002. Ex-BR diesels come next, listed in sequence according to their early BR 'D' numbers. These are followed by the diesel multiple units and railbuses. The Worth Valley's fleet of industrial steam locomotives come next. In this category are the two ex-Lancashire & Yorkshire tanks, sold out of service by the LMS before Nationalisation. These too are listed in numerical sequence. Industrial diesel locomotives follow and the last part of the book deals with three steam locomotives built for the British and American military authorities during the last war.

Today, it is a sheer delight to travel by train along the Worth Valley, and perhaps linger awhile, and soak up the atmosphere, at some of the stations, or wander around the various museum sites. The KWVR forms a glorious monument to our railway heritage, but at the same time, provides a valuable service to the community at large, both socially and economically.

The class 25s while in BR service often worked in multiple. With No 25 161 assisting in front, the future KWVR example No 25 059, is seen hauling a long link of westbound roadstone hoppers through Westbury station on 17th September 1975. Also, of interest are the galaxy of ex-GWR lower quadrant semaphore signals, along with the signalbox on the left. Tom Heavyside

No 5775

The Great Western Railway built pannier tanks, with an 0-6-0 wheel configuration, in profusion. Indeed, the type was almost synonymous with the GWR. They were used universally throughout the system for yard shunting, light goods traffic, branch line and stopping passenger services. Later, under BR, during the 1950s, every shed on the Western Region had at least one of the type on its allocation list.

The 57xx series were designed by Collett, and the first emerged from Swindon Works in 1929. Ultimately they became the largest class of engines built solely for use in Britain, the last

and 863rd example not being constructed until 1950. No 5775 was released from Swindon in September 1929, and was put to work from Neath shed in South Wales.

At the time of Nationalisation, on 1st January 1948, No 5775 was on the books of the former Rhondda & Swansea Bay Railway shed at Danygraig, Swansea, coded 87C. It remained there until October 1952 when it moved to Carmarthen (87G). Its last reallocation under BR came in March 1956 when it was transferred to Pontypool Road (86G).

From the mid-1950s much of the work undertaken by the panniers was progressively taken over by diesel power, while many became redundant due to branch line and station clo-

Above: **An early view of No 5775, at Neath shed on 14th April 1933. The number is painted on the front buffer.** P J T Reed

Opposite page bottom: **No 5775 reposes in the shed yard at Pontypool Road, its last BR shed, on 10th February 1957. It bears the original BR lion and wheel emblem on the tank side. Another four 0-6-0PTs are in view including, on the right, No 7720 from Aberdare (86J) shed.** Industrial Railway Society / Brian Webb collection

Below: **While BR finished with steam in August 1968, London Transport continued to utilise their former GWR 0-6-0PTs. On 2nd July 1969 No 5775, bereft of its former BR identification plates and emblem, now running as No L89, is seen shunting some engineers wagons and a couple of brake vans at Kensington.** David Idle

sures. However the modernisation plans took time to effect Pontypool Road, for the shed still had 25 0-6-0PTs on its books in July 1962. But for No 5775 the end of life on BR was nigh, being withdrawn in January 1963. Only Nos 5749 and 5787 outlived it from the initial batch of 100.

During the mid-1950s London Transport sought to replace some of its ageing steam fleet, which was used mainly on engineering trains. Discarded BR 0-6-0PTs seemed the answer and, in October 1956, LT took delivery of 57xx class No 7711. Over the next seven years they purchased a further 12, the last of these being No 5775, in July 1963. It was repainted in LT maroon livery and numbered L89.

At the end of the 1960s the LT panniers became surplus to requirements for a second time, No 5775 moving to the Keighley & Worth Valley Railway in January 1970. Never an engine to be at the forefront of things in its GWR, BR, or LT days, spending the vast majority of its time on somewhat humdrum, but nevertheless, vital duties, this was set to change dramatically, following its arrival at Haworth.

During the spring of 1970 No 5775 was catapulted into the limelight, when it was cast in a starring role in the feature film 'The Railway Children'. At the head of the old gentleman's train in a fictitious GN&SR brown livery, it has since been seen by countless millions of cinema and television viewers.

For many years the locomotive plied the Worth Valley in its London Transport guise as No L89, while, for a brief spell, in 1990, it was returned to its 'Railway Children' colours for the 20th anniversary of the production. It has since resumed its normal identity as BR No 5775 .

No 5775 is one of 24 ex-GWR 0-6-0PTs which have been preserved, including 16 members of the 57xx class.

No 30072

This page: **Employed on Target No 8, No 30072 shunts a light load of four wagons at Southampton Docks on 11th July 1962.**
Ron Herbert

Opposite page: **No 30072 at Guildford shed, in company with Maunsell class N 2-6-0 No 31858, also allocated to Guildford, on 12th June 1965. The half-roundhouse shed building can be seen behind No 31858.**
David Idle

At the end of the Second World War, the Southern Railway needed to find some replacement power for a fleet of elderly Adams B4 class 0-4-0Ts, employed at Southampton Docks, as these were in need of urgent repair. A powerful, short wheel-based locomotive was required, and the British-built 'Austerity' 0-6-0ST design was rejected in favour of the USA Army Transportation Corps 0-6-0T, which had become surplus to requirements following the cessation of hostilities in 1945.

The USATC had 382 of these 0-6-0Ts constructed between 1942 and 1944, 150 by Porter's, 123 by Vulcan Iron Works and 109 from Davenport's. From 1943, after arriving from America, some were utilised in Britain at Army bases and collieries, before the majority were shipped to the Continent. After the war, many remained there for many years, serving in France, Greece, and Yugoslavia. The 42 members of the class which remained in Britain were eventually dumped near Newbury Racecourse pending a decision as to their future.

The Southern Railway decided to purchase 15 of these at a price of £2,500 each. They were all at Eastleigh Works by the end of 1946. During 1947 14 were progressively made serviceable and one was used as a spares source and never officially added to stock. Some modifications were made, not least the fitting of steam heating equipment, very necessary for warming the stock required for the numerous boat trains emanating from Southampton.

The SR numbered them 61 to 74, No 72 starting work in April 1947. It was then only four years old, having commenced life as WD No 1973, after manufacture at Vulcan Iron Works, Wilkes-Barre, Pennsylvania, as works No 4446, in 1943.

The engines, with a 10ft wheel-base and a nominal tractive effort of 21,600lb, proved very useful machines. The Southern Railway designated them the USA class – very appropriate in view of their many non-British features.

These included three large domes, a stove-pipe chimney, bar frames and no running-plate, along with outside valve-gear and rods driving the rear axle.

After Nationalisation the class was renumbered 30061-74, and they remained attached to Southampton Docks shed. Their position was not challenged until 1962, when some diesel shunters arrived to take over. A few were then retained by Eastleigh shed and still used occasionally at the Docks, while others were transferred to Departmental stock. However No 30072 was found a new home, at Guildford shed (70C), from February 1963.

At Guildford No 30072 replaced an ageing class B4 0-4-0T No 30089, on shed pilot duties. Guildford shed, a half-roundhouse, was on a very cramped site, and a short wheel-based engine was required to manoeuvre out-of-steam engines around the yard. No 30072 was retained for this humble task until the very end of Southern Region steam on 9th July 1967. It did,

however, have one moment of glory, on 4th February 1967, when it hauled a two-coach special from Guildford to Dorking, in connection with the Railway Enthusiasts Club annual dinner. While club members enjoyed the festive occasion, No 30072 was serviced at Redhill shed.

On Sunday 9th July 1967, in common with many other redundant Southern engines, No 30072 made its melancholy way west to Salisbury shed for storage. This was a convenient location for South Wales scrap-metal merchants to view and assess yet more prospective fodder for their yards. Fortuitously No 30072 escaped their clutches, BR accepting a private bid for the 0-6-0T, which enabled the engine to move to previously uncharted territory on the KWVR.

The next year it had the honour of hauling the KWVR opening special, in tandem with No 41241, on 29th June 1968. The USA tank sported a somewhat controversial brown livery,

a silver smokebox, with 'Worth Valley' emblazoned on the tank sides and carried the number 72. From 1976 to 1987 the engine operated as an oil-burner.

Today the engine is more popularly painted in a smart green lined livery, even though plain black was its customary colour in BR days. It also carries its BR number. Three more of the SR's 'USA' tanks have been preserved, while the Swanage Railway has imported one from Yugoslavia, the latter having been built to the original wartime design as late as 1960.

Above: **In June 1964 No 30072 was despatched to Eastleigh Works for overhaul. Before returning to Guildford it is viewed at Eastleigh shed, in company with her Eastleigh-based sister No 30067, on 8th September. No 30067 went for scrap following its withdrawal in July 1967.**
Gavin Morrison

No 34092 *City of Wells*

One of the most innovative, if controversial, locomotive engineers of the twentieth century was O V S Bulleid. After appointment as chief mechanical engineer of the Southern Railway in October 1937, his first design was the 'Merchant Navy' class 3-cylinder Pacific. The first member of the class, No 21C1 *Channel Packet*, began steaming trials in February 1941. Hitherto Britain's railways had seen nothing like it, either mechanically or aesthetically.

Most noticeable was the box-like shape of the outer casing. The other main visible parts, the wheels, were also different to the normal spoked design, Bulleid patenting a boxpok type in liaison with Firth Brown.

Hidden from view was the welded steel firebox, as opposed to the more normal copper type, serving a boiler pressed to 280lb, later reduced to 250lb, and what proved to be a very troublesome feature – a chain-linked motion totally enclosed in an oil bath, set between the frames. The engine crews were pleased with the cab layout, power-operated firedoor, rocking grates and hopper-type ashpans.

Following the introduction of the 'Merchant Navy' class, Bulleid turned his attention to a smaller engine, which after much discussion evolved as a scaled-down version of the MNs. The resultant 'West Country / Battle of Britain' class Pacifics, the first of which did not appear, due to war-time austerity conditions, until May 1945, tipped the scales at 86 tons, against the 94 tons of the MNs. A maximum axle loading of 18 tons 15 cwt meant they could travel almost anywhere on the Southern Railway.

Bedecked in full 'Golden Arrow' regalia – headboard, British and French flags, and a large arrow along the boiler side – *City of Wells* roars through Chelsfield, along former South Eastern & Chatham Railway metals, leading the down service from London Victoria to Folkestone Harbour in September 1959. Derek Cross

Between them the SR and BR built 110 WC / BBs, the most numerous Pacific type to run in Britain, and far more than could be employed to their full potential on Southern lines. Following Nationalisation, and with other Regions unwilling to accept them on a permanent basis, due to their many non-standard features, they were often used on light duties. During the 1950s and early '60s, they could be seen daily, west of Exeter, ambling along single-track branches with two or three coaches in tow. Conversely, when the need arose, they could competently deputise for the larger 'Merchant Navy' class.

No 34092 was one of the final batch of 20 ordered from Brighton Works in March 1949, leaving there in September of that year, in the by then standard lined Brunswick green livery. It was sent immediately to Stewarts Lane shed (73A), where it remained throughout the 1950s.

Two months later it made the journey to the small Somerset cathedral city of Wells where, on 25th November, it was formally named *Wells* by the Mayor. The following March it was renamed *City of Wells* – more akin to the nomenclature adopted by the LMS for the 'Coronation' class Pacifics. Renaming made No 34092 quite distinctive, since the rest of the 'West Countrys' only carried the name of a city, town, or locality.

During the 1950s *City of Wells* settled down to working trains out of London to the Kent coast, along with her sisters allocated to 73A. The shed usually had between 13 and 17 of the class on its books at this time. In its early days, and then again in the late 1950s, No 34092 was often called upon to haul the prestigious 'Golden Arrow' service out of London Victoria.

With safety valves lifting, No 34092 *City of Wells* takes water outside Stewarts Lane, its home shed for 11 years, before reversing to Victoria station, to take charge of a passenger train on 25th May 1958. R C Riley

During its last summer of BR use, *City of Wells*, coasts into Bournemouth Central, with the 3.00pm Bournemouth West to Waterloo, on 3rd August 1964. The buildings of Bournemouth shed (71B) can be seen on the right of the locomotive. Ivo Peters

Further honours bestowed on *City of Wells* during this period came first on 18th April 1956, when it was chosen to haul the train of seven Pullman cars conveying the Soviet supremos Bulganin and Kruschev, from Portsmouth Harbour to Victoria, at the start of their historic visit to England and then on 16th July 1956 it had charge of a Royal Train carrying King Feisal of Iraq, from Dover to Victoria.

In 1961, with the completion of electrification work on the lines to the Kent coast, the need for steam on the Eastern Section was much reduced. Thus No 34092 was despatched from Stewarts Lane for the last time in May 1961, to a new home at Salisbury (72B).

At the end of 1961 Salisbury shed possessed 14 light Pacifics, including six of the 60 which were rebuilt along more conventional lines. No 34092 was used mainly along the former LSWR main line to London Waterloo and west to Exeter. While at Salisbury No 34092 received what was to be the penultimate overhaul to a non-rebuilt WC/BB class, at Eastleigh Works, in November 1962. Work on No 34007 *Wadebridge* was completed the following month.

With the need for steam locomotives on the Southern Region continually declining, No 34092 was withdrawn in November 1964, having recorded 502,864 miles. Of her classmates only No 34091 *Weymouth* covered less ground, with 469,073 miles to her credit.

During March 1965 *City of Wells* arrived at Woodham Bros yard at Barry, South Wales, ostensibly for scrapping. As is well documented this was not to be the fate of the vast majority of Woodham's purchases and, in October 1971, No 34092 left Barry for more northern climes, to a new home on the KWVR. It was the first of 18 WC/BB Pacifics, among them eight still in original condition, to be hauled away from Barry. In addition to these, two other light Bulleid Pacifics went directly from BR service into preservation.

After renovation No 34092 was used throughout the 1980s, both on the Worth Valley, and on numerous main line excursions, before a further overhaul became due. In 1985 a Giesl ejector was fitted, a device which improves the exhaust blast, increasing power output, in addition to

reducing fuel consumption. *City of Wells* is not the first Bulleid Pacific to sport a Giesl ejector, BR satisfactorily experimenting with one on No 34064 *Fighter Command* from May 1964. The development came too late in the day for it to be worthwhile installing widely on BR steam locos, the only other BR locomotive to carry one being BR Standard 9F 2-10-0 No 92250.

The oblong chimney, which is an integral part of the Giesl system, often has a detrimental effect on an engine's appearance. With *City of Wells* this is not the case, since it is mainly hidden from view by the outer casing. Thus while now a stronger engine than when in BR ownership, outwardly it looks very much as it did in the 1950s, when it regularly headed for the Kent coast, in charge of the 'Golden Arrow' or the more mundane services on these lines.

***City of Wells* struggles for adhesion leaving Templecombe, with the 11.45am SO Waterloo-Exmouth service on 13th July 1963. This station, on the ex-LSWR main line to the West Country, which provided an interchange with trains on the former S&D route from Bath to Bournemouth, closed on 7th March 1966. Following much local pressure the station reopened on 3rd October 1983, to be served by Waterloo-Exeter trains.**
Hugh Ballantyne

No 41241

In 1946 H G Ivatt introduced on the LMS a light-weight class 2 2-6-2T. They were virtually to the same specifications as the 2-6-0s in the 64xx series, first built in the same year, except for the addition of side-tanks, coal bunker and a trailing axle in place of a tender. Both variants incorporated rocking grates, self-emptying ashpans and self-cleaning smokeboxes.

Only ten 2-6-2Ts were constructed by the LMS but, following Nationalisation, production continued until 1952, by which time the class was 130 strong. They were all built at Crewe, except for the last ten, Nos 41320-9, for which Derby was responsible. The class became widely scattered throughout the London Midland and Southern Regions. In 1956 they had 91 and 35 respectively, with the remaining four residing on the Western Region.

Their main forte was local passenger and branch line work, some being adapted for push-pull working whereby, in one direction, the driver could operate a set of coaches from the leading carriage, with the engine propelling at the rear by means of suitable connections. The fireman remained on the locomotive at all times. This saved much valuable time at terminal stations, due to the engine not having to run round its train after every journey. In later years some of the class acted as station pilots, as at London Waterloo and Stockport Edgeley.

During the 1950s, push-pull Ivatt 2-6-2Ts regularly operated the Keighley-Oxenhope branch, and there is much photographic evidence of Nos 41273, 41325 and 41326 employed on the line. They were made redundant when the service was taken over by diesel multiple units from 13th June 1960.

No 41241 left Crewe in September 1949, bound for Southern Region Bath Green Park shed (71G). Here it was used on services to Bristol Temple Meads via Mangotsfield, and occasionally along the erstwhile, and much lamented, Somerset & Dorset Railway, with a local evening stopping train which went as far as Binegar. During the summer of 1951 it was loaned for a short spell to the small ex-S&D shed at Highbridge (71J).

Much to the chagrin of many people, from 1st February 1958, the northern section of the S&D was placed in the hands of the Western Region, including the shed at Bath. The following summer No 41241's time at Bath (then coded 82F) was interrupted for three months when it went to Bristol Barrow Road (82E).

In October 1959 No 41241 left Bath – this time permanently, for Wellington in Shropshire (84H), where it worked local services such as those to Crewe and Much Wenlock. While at Wellington the Ivatt witnessed yet another regional boundary change when, in September 1963, that part of the Western Region became London Midland territory. Thereafter, in January 1964, No 41241 moved to Leamington Spa (2L). It returned to Wellington in June – then coded 2M, for just one week, before travelling to North Wales for pastures new.

No 41241 spent its first month in Wales at Bangor (6H), before going to Croes Newydd shed (6C), in Wrexham, at the end of July 1964. It spent almost a year there, leaving in June 1965 for another short sojourn near the coast, at Llandudno Junction (6G). However in mid-August it was on the move once more, this time to the Yorkshire Dales, to Skipton (10G), where it was to eke out its BR days.

The engine was withdrawn by BR in December 1966. From Skipton it was just a short hop down the Aire Valley, to the embryonic Keighley & Worth Valley Railway where No 41241 was destined to haul the reopening special on 29th June 1968, albeit in an uncharacteristic maroon livery, double-heading with USA 0-6-0T No 30072. It has since reverted to its more familiar BR lined black.

No 41241 spent its BR days working some quite picturesque lines, a suitable prelude to its current career on the Worth Valley. Three more of these excellent machines are preserved elsewhere.

Opposite page: **No 41241 leads a tender-first Ivatt class 4 2-6-0 No 43039 at Bath Green Park at the head of the 10.00am all stations service to Bristol Temple Meads on 21st June 1952. The double-heading of this train was to facilitate the return of No 43039 to Bristol.** Ivo Peters

This page, top: **On a bitterly cold winter morning, with a couple of coaches in tow, No 41241 heads for its birthplace, as it restarts from Audlem with the 10.08 am Wellington-Crewe service on 30th December 1960. Passenger services along this former Great Western Railway route finished on 9th September 1963.** Hugh Ballantyne

Right: **A time warp at Much Wenlock in the early 1960s. No 41241 runs-round its train before heading back to Wellington. Passenger services from this ex-GWR station were withdrawn from 23rd July 1962.** Trevor Radway

In its last months of BR ownership, on 7th September 1966, No 41241 stands outside Skipton shed, ready to move a solitary coal wagon and a brake-van. On the smokebox door can be seen painted the code 6H, that of Bangor shed, to which No 41241 was allocated for only one month, in June 1964. The days when steam engines could almost be guaranteed to be carrying a correct shedplate, had regrettably past, indicative of official attitudes towards steam traction at this time. Hamish Stevenson

No 43924

The Midland Railway's small engine policy, for both passenger and goods work, is well known. Continuing a long line of 0-6-0 designs for the company, Fowler introduced in 1911, what was to become a standard class for freight workings. In all 772 were produced, the last not until 1941 by the LMS. A development of the earlier inside-cylindered Midland class 3 Johnson design, with a superheated boiler and a nominal tractive effort of 24,555lb, they were very steady reliable machines and easy to maintain. The Midland built 192 of these class 4s, prior to Grouping, plus another five for the Somerset & Dorset Joint Railway. The London Midland & Scottish Rail-

way, who adopted the MR power classification system, ordered a further 575 4Fs, although these had left hand drive, as opposed to the MR engines, which were driven from the right. Four main railway workshops, and four private locomotive builders participated in their construction.

As an indication of their widespread use it should be noted that in the spring of 1956, 71 London Midland Region sheds had an allocation. In addition 11 Scottish Region sheds had some responsibility for them, as did two Eastern Region depots, Gorton (39A) and Peterborough Spital (35C). Traditionally some were still based at Bath Green Park (71G) and Templecombe (71H), on the ex-Somerset & Dorset Railway, then part of the Southern Region. Although principally employed on loose-coupled freight dia-

grams, they were also used to haul the occasional passenger train.

Built at the Midland Railway headquarters at Derby, in October 1920, No 3924 was first allocated to Wellingborough shed. It spent the next ten years mainly working well-laden slow-moving coal trains south to London, and returning empty wagons to East Midlands coal mines.

No 3924 is seen in its very early days, at Kentish Town shed, London, having worked south from Wellingborough. Note the Johnson six-wheel tender, the Midland Railway Wyvern crest on the cabside, and just discernible on the upper cabside is a small brass numeral '4', indicating its power classification. R L Inns collection

From March 1930 home for No 3924 was the massive Saltley shed (21A), in the Birmingham suburbs, before it moved to Gloucester Barnwood (22B) in July 1937. Gloucester men must have been well pleased with their acquisition, for it stayed there 25 years, working the ex-MR lines north and south of the city.

Finally, in September 1962, No 43924, as it became following Nationalisation, being renumbered in February 1949, was transferred to Bristol Barrow Road (82E), for three years, before it was condemned in July 1965. Three months later it made what was purported to be its last journey, to Woodham's scrapyard at Barry, South Wales.

However, No 43924 was destined to have an important place in the annals of railway history, for in September 1968 it was hauled from Woodham's yard, to join the growing stud of engines on the recently opened KWVR. At the time this was a brave, pioneering, move by the Midland 4F Society, for never before had an engine been rescued from a scrapyard.

No 43924 was, of course, just the first of the Woodham's owned engines to flee the threat of the cutters torch, and over the next 22 years preservationists removed a further 212 locomotives from the yard, a quite extraordinary achievement.

While No 43924 is the only one of the original Midland Railway class 4 0-6-0s preserved, three of the LMS series survive. Two of these were also resuscitated from Woodham's, while No 44027, presently based at the Midland Railway Centre, Butterley, forms part of the National collection.

A portrait of No 43924 outside Gloucester Barnwood shed on 27th September 1953. The 4F is now coupled to a much more familiar Fowler tender but note that the locomotive has retained the small MR brass '4' on the upper cabside, and has acquired the LMS/BR power classification '4F' painted above the cabside number. Brian Hilton

Above: **Three months before it was transferred away from Gloucester Barnwood shed, after 25 years residence there, No 43924 has charge of a short goods, on the High Orchard branch from Gloucester Docks, during June 1962.** W Potter

Right: **With only three months of life remaining in BR capital stock, No 43924 rests inside the roundhouse at Bristol Barrow Road shed on 20th March 1965. On its right is an unidentified double-chimneyed BR class 9F 2-10-0, its smokebox door numberplate having been removed.**
David Idle

No 45212

The Stanier LMS taper-boilered class 5 4-6-0s, introduced in 1934, was one of the most successful designs to grace Britain's railways. In traffic they proved able to handle, with almost consummate ease, both express and stopping passenger trains alike, and were equally at home on freight turns of every description.

The first engine put together was No 5020, built by the Vulcan Foundry, Newton-le-Willows, Lancashire, in August 1934. By May 1951 there were no less than 842 in service. In addition to Vulcan, Armstrong Whitworth laid frames for the class, as did the LMS/BR works at Crewe, Derby and Horwich. There were some detail differences between the batches, while some of the latter engines were fitted with various experimental features, such as Caprotti valve gear and Timken roller-bearings.

During the 1950s they roamed far and wide. Indeed, the outline of the 'Black 5s' was familiar from the far North of Scotland, where they were the mainstay of Highland line services, (Inverness shed had 33 and Perth 75 in 1950), to the South Coast of England, at Bournemouth, which they usually reached via the Somerset & Dorset line.

At this time, due to their widespread dispersal and the large number in service, they were certainly not the enthusiasts' favourite, as they appeared with almost monotonous regularity in many areas. However, engine crews viewed them in a different light, as they were free runners and strong on the inclines.

No 5212 entered traffic in November 1935, having been built by Armstrong Whitworth, at Newcastle-upon-Tyne. In common with the early members of the class it had a shorter fire-box than some of the examples constructed later, along with a domeless boiler.

No 5212 went straight to Low Moor shed (25F), near Bradford, where it was used frequently on trans-Pennine diagrams over the difficult Calder Valley route to Manchester and Liverpool. From the records it appears Low Moor made very good use of the locomotive, for it travelled over 50,000 miles in each of the years 1936 to 1938. It subsequently averaged approx 35,400 miles per annum during the rest of its stay in Yorkshire.

In November 1947, just prior to Nationalisation, No 5212 moved to Fleetwood (24F). Here it received its BR number 45212, in October 1948. It stayed at Fleetwood until October 1964, during which time it continued to visit Manchester with semi-fast passenger trains from the fishing port. No doubt, it was also used, from time to

Opposite page: **In a line of four Stanier 'Black 5s' stored at Carlisle Upperby shed (12B), No 45212 stands next to No 45253, on 1st April 1967. Behind is 'Britannia' Pacific No 70051, shorn of its** *Firth of Forth* **nameplates.** Derek Cross

Above: **No 45212 provides a stirring sight viewed from the well known Shap Wells mound, as it grapples with the 1 in 75 climb to Shap summit, with an eleven coach special returning to Glasgow from Blackpool on 25th September 1967. At the rear, one of Tebay shed's BR Standard class 4 4-6-0s provides welcome assistance. At the end of 1967 regular steam working over Shap came to an end with the closure of Carlisle Kingmoor and Tebay sheds to steam, No 45212 being shedded at the former at this time.** Hamish Stevenson

time, on some of the many fish trains which originated there.

During the 1950s No 45212 averaged 29,055 miles per annum. At the end of 1960 it had recorded 856,187 miles. After this no further mileage details were logged by BR and there must be a question mark, as to whether or not it surpassed the one million mark by the time of its withdrawal in 1968.

From October 1964 No 45212 was shedded successively at Carnforth (10A), Speke Junction (8C) from March 1965, back to Carnforth in June 1965, and then to Carlisle Kingmoor (12A) in September of that year.

When Carlisle Kingmoor closed at the end of 1967, No 45212 was transferred to Lostock Hall (10D), one of 151 'Black 5s', out of 359 standard gauge steam locomotives retained by BR at the start of 1968. It was rostered by 10D on some of

the last remaining passenger turns, which radiated from Preston to Blackpool, Liverpool and Manchester, as well as on various freight duties around Lancashire.

Saturday 3rd August 1968 was the last day of scheduled steam on ordinary services on BR. The next-to-last train was the 20.50 Preston-Blackpool South, the rear portion of the 17.05 from London Euston. Appropriately, in view of its long association with the Fylde, the Lostock Hall foreman deputed No 45212 to head this train. A large throng witnessed its departure to a battery of flash guns, the carriages packed to capacity with enthusiasts, savouring, what to them, were very precious moments.

On its return to Preston just one final task remained for No 45212 – to shunt two terminating sleeping cars off the 23.45 from Euston, into a bay platform, during the early hours of Sunday morning. Thus No 45212 can rightfully claim the dubious distinction of being the last steam locomotive employed by BR on a normal service train, albeit just a short shunting movement, carrying a few slumbering passengers.

This duty completed, the Stanier 4-6-0 then made its way quietly and with little fuss, compared to the earlier proceedings, back to Lostock Hall shed, where the fire was dropped for what was thought would be the last time.

However, two months later it was to take up residence, on the then recently opened KWVR, not far away from its original home at Low Moor shed, Bradford. It should be noted that the engine carries a later standard type domed boiler, acquired earlier in its BR career, rather than the original domeless variety. No 45212 is one of 18 Stanier 'Black 5s' still extant.

Left: **On the last day of scheduled steam working on normal services, 3rd August 1968, No 45212 awaits the 'right away' from Preston station with the 20.50 to Blackpool South, the penultimate steam passenger train on BR. A home-made headboard has been fixed, somewhat precariously, to the smokebox door by local enthusiasts to commemorate the event. It reads 'Preston to Blackpool. 3rd August 1968. The End of Steam. Farewell'.** Peter J Fitton

Below: **With the photographer wisely sheltering under the station canopy, during a torrential downpour, No 45212 runs through Blackburn with a long link of empty mineral wagons destined for Rose Grove, Burnley, in July 1968.** Allan Heyes

No 45596 *Bahamas*

When William A Stanier was appointed Chief Mechanical Engineer of the LM&SR, in January 1932, there were pressing problems in the motive power department.

Within a short time he was supervising the design of new 4-6-0s, a type he knew well from his experience with his previous employers, the Great Western Railway. Thus in 1934, there emerged, not only the first of the 'Black 5s', in August, as already described, but four months earlier in April, the prototype three-cylinder taper-boiler class 5XP No 5552, had been built at Crewe Works. The class were later known as 'Jubilees', following the naming of No 5552 *Silver Jubilee* in May 1935, although the locomotive named and numbered as such was built as No 5642, identities having been exchanged.

The 5XPs were a Stanier development of the Fowler 'Patriot' class 4-6-0s, and by December 1936 191 were in service. Crewe Works produced 131, and Derby 10, while the remaining 50 were ordered from the Glasgow-based North British Locomotive Company. They had 6ft 9in diameter driving wheels as against those of 6ft fitted to the 'Black 5s', and were marginally more powerful, with a tractive effort of 26,610lb – the '5s' having 25,455lb nominally available. They were intended for use on main line passenger trains and fitted-freights.

The first batches entered traffic with dome-less boilers, which, in the main, were quickly replaced by a domed version, as fitted new to the final batch of 78. Once some early problems had been rectified, they gave good service, almost until the dying days of steam on BR.

As a guide to their sphere of operation, it is worth noting that in April 1956, by which time BR had reclassified them 6P5F, 22 sheds had an allocation. They ranged from Camden (1B) and Kentish Town (14B), in London, with 8 and 13 respectively, Bristol Barrow Road (22A) in the west with 12, to Perth (63A) in the north which had three. Leeds Holbeck (20A) and Carlisle Kingmoor (68A) had the most, each with 18, although Crewe North had 17, and Preston (10B) only two. At this time the class ran in BR standard lined Brunswick green livery, which had replaced the LMS crimson lake of earlier years.

Trailing nine 'blood and custard' liveried coaches, *Bahamas* replenishes its Fowler tender from Dillicar water troughs, just south of Tebay, on the West Coast main line, when on an up express, on 10th May 1956. At this time it has a single chimney and was shedded at Carlisle Upperby. D M C Hepburne-Scott / Rail Archive Stephenson

No 5596 left the North British, Queens Park Works, in January 1935, carrying a price tag of £5,866 including tender. It was named *Bahamas*, without ceremony, on 8th June 1936, and received a replacement domed boiler in November 1937. During the early part of its life *Bahamas* was quite nomadic, its LMS/BR permanent allocations being as follows:

January	1935	Crewe North
May	1935	Preston
January	1936	Aston
July	1937	Camden
August	1937	Willesden
December	1937	Crewe North
July	1938	Camden
August	1938	Kentish Town
September	1939	Derby
March	1940	Grimesthorpe, Sheffield
September	1941	Millhouses, Sheffield
April	1947	Bristol Barrow Road
October	1947	Crewe North
December	1948	Edge Hill, Liverpool
February	1956	Carlisle Upperby
July	1962	Stockport Edgeley

Bahamas started and ended its LMS/BR career attached to Stanier-designed 4,000 gallon tenders, but from 1936 to 1940, and then from 1946 to 1960, it ran paired with Fowler straight-sided 3,500 gallon tenders.

When the London Midland Region stopped logging detailed mileage statistics, at the end of 1960, No 45596, as it had been renumbered by BR in May 1948, had travelled 1,273,408 miles, an average of 48,977 per annum. The highest in any one year was 72,474 in 1939.

Perhaps the most significant development in the history of *Bahamas*, was the fitting of a double blastpipe and chimney at Crewe Works in May 1961. Previously four other 'Jubilees' had carried double-chimneys, three for very short

Here *Bahamas* has just arrived at Birmingham New Street on 29th June 1957, with the previous night's 11.45pm service from Edinburgh Princes Street.
Michael Mensing

periods, although No (4)5742 *Connaught* retained one from 1940 to 1955. *Bahamas* was the only one so adapted in the 1960s which gave the engine a unique appearance compared to its sisters, a distinction evident to this day.

Bahamas was discarded by BR in July 1966, and purchased the following year, by the Bahamas Locomotive Society. Despatched to the Hunslet Engine Company, Leeds, for a full overhaul, it was outshopped from there in March 1968, bearing LMS crimson lake livery as No 5596. After a period in storage at Bury, it arrived at the fledgling Dinting Railway Centre in November 1968.

Since being preserved *Bahamas* has headed many main line excursions on BR, and visited a number of private lines, but since the disbandment of the Dinting site in 1990, the KWVR has been regarded as home. Today it operates as BR No 45596 in lined Brunswick green livery, one of only four 'Jubilees' still in existence.

Top right: **On a pleasant autumnal morning, *Bahamas* threads the Glasgow suburbs, at Bellahouston, with a local from Kilmarnock, on 11th October 1958. This train ran via Dalry and Paisley Canal, over former Glasgow & South Western Railway metals, before terminating at Glasgow St Enoch. The train includes LMS built articulated carriages.** Hamish Stevenson

Right: **In unfamiliar territory for a Carlisle Upperby-based engine, on 4th September 1960, *Bahamas*, by this time coupled to a Stanier tender but still with a single-chimney, hurries the Sunday 4.00pm Manchester to London St Pancras service along the Midland main line, at Syston, north of Leicester. Syston station can be seen just beyond the bridge in the right background. There can be little doubt that many local trainspotters along the route would be pleased by the appearance of *Bahamas* in these parts!** John Stretton

Above: **A fine portrait of No 45596 *Bahamas*, at Farnley Junction shed (55C), on 4th September 1963. The double-chimney profile, and its 9B Stockport Edgeley shedplate, are clearly seen. On the left is Gorton-allocated ex-WD 8F 2-8-0 No 90558.** Gavin Morrison

Left: ***Bahamas* shunts Copley Hill yard, Leeds, on 22nd April 1965. The diagonal yellow stripe on the cabside was meant as a clear warning that the engine was prohibited from running along the electrified West Coast main line south of Crewe, due to insufficient clearances. Note too the oblong red on white flash-warning signs, placed at strategic positions, to warn footplate staff of the inherent dangers when working under overhead wires.** Gavin Morrison

No 47279

Following the Grouping of the railways in 1923, the London Midland & Scottish Railway quickly realised the need to replace many of the elderly shunting locomotives inherited from the constituent companies. To expedite matters they decided to perpetuate an already proven Midland Railway Johnson inside-cylindered 0-6-0T design of 1899, but with some detail alterations and improvements.

The LMS placed orders for 407 of these engines with five private locomotive building firms. They were delivered between 1924 and 1929. A further 15 were constructed later in their own workshops, at Horwich, in 1931. They became popularly known as 'Jinties'.

The class were widely scattered throughout the LMS, and later BR's London Midland Region. Trip freights and shunting work was their forte, and they were often prominent at large stations as the duty pilot engine. For many years some were based at Bromsgrove shed for banking Birmingham bound trains up the notorious Lickey incline, sometimes three of them, in tandem, noisily lending their weight, at the rear of a particularly heavy train. Similar work was done on the Somerset & Dorset line, on the climb to Masbury summit. They did a little passenger work, particularly over former LNWR lines in the Swansea area, a few being push-pull fitted.

The Keighley 'Jinty' left the Vulcan Foundry, Newton-le-Willows, in 1924, works No 3736. It was originally LMS No 7119, this being amended to No 7279 under the LMS 1934 renumbering scheme. It became BR No 47279 in September 1949.

In its first guise as No 7119, the future KWVR 'Jinty' shunts at an unknown location, when but a comparative youngster.
T G Hepburn / Rail Archive Stephenson

Its early years were spent shunting the vast coal marshalling yards at Toton, before moving to Nottingham in May 1934 and then Wellingborough in May 1938. It remained at the latter shed until August 1957, when it was transferred to Bedford (15D), before returning to Wellingborough (15A) in August 1963.

No 47279's long association with Midland Railway territory was finally severed in November 1963, when it made the long journey north to Workington. Based at 12D, it stayed at this Cumbrian Coast outpost for just over two years, shunting locally mined coal and the output from the steelworks, before being relocated to Merseyside.

No 47279 took up its duties at Aintree (8L) in December 1965. In November 1966 it moved to Sutton Oak (8G), only to be taken out of service at the end of the year.

By 1967 Woodham Bros were casting their eye far and wide in their search for suitable scrap metal, and fortunately their bid for No 47279 was accepted by the LMR authorities. In June 1967 the engine arrived at Barry, South Wales, for what was to prove a 12 year sojourn, quietly rotting in the salty sea air.

After the appropriate cheque had been handed over to Woodham's, No 47279 arrived at Haworth in August 1979. It is one of ten 'Jinties' saved for posterity.

Below: **On 18th April 1957 No 47279 is engaged on shunting duties, on the opposite side of the Midland main line to Wellingborough shed. Outside the depot can be seen an unidentified Stanier 8F 2-8-0 and, on the right, BR 9F 2-10-0 No 92059, both types being very familiar on Midland main line goods traffic at this time.** K C H Fairey

Opposite page: **Steam escapes furiously from the safety valves of No 47279, while working at Bedford, adjacent to the ex-Midland Railway line to Hitchin, on 18th September 1961.** Michael Mensing

No 48431

The history of the LMS class 8F 2-8-0s is complex. Designed by Stanier, the first was built at Crewe in 1935, as part of his plan to update and standardise the locomotive stock of the LMS.

The 8Fs incorporated many features common to the 'Black 5s', but their smaller 4ft 8½in diameter driving wheels provided an increased tractive effort of 32,440lb. The '5s' had 6ft wheels and a tractive effort of 25,455lb. Both classes weighed 72 tons 2 cwt without tender. The lower running plate of the 8Fs gave them an easily identifiable outline.

During the 1930s the need for replacement heavy freight engines on the LMS was nothing like as urgent as that for passenger and mixed traffic types, and by 1939 only 126 8Fs had been built. Like the early class 5s, the first 12 had domeless boilers, but the rest were fitted from new with the domed type.

With the onset of World War Two the situation changed, and there was soon a dire need for more heavy freight engines, both in Britain, and for projected use overseas.

The War Department, realising their attributes, were quick to requisition some 8Fs from the LMS, and from 1940 to 1942 ordered and took delivery of a further 208 constructed by Beyer Peacock and the North British Locomotive Company.

Left: **Treading the sea wall at Teignmouth, between Exeter and Newton Abbot, No 48431 prepares to turn inland, approaching Teignmouth station, with a down freight on 15th July 1959. At this time the 8F was based at St Philip's Marsh shed.** Bill Ashcroft

No 8431 emerged from Swindon Works in March 1944, one of 80 built by the Great Western Railway, and which, officially, were then loaned to the GWR. Following GWR tradition the number was painted on the front buffer-beam, rather than displayed on a smokebox numberplate as was the LMS practice. Its early years were spent attached to Newton Abbot and Gloucester sheds.

In 1947 the GWR Stanier 8Fs were handed over to the LMS, No 8431 being allocated to Royston shed (20C), near Barnsley, from March of that year. The prefix 4 was added to the number by BR in November 1949, and in September 1950 it was among 19 8Fs domiciled at Royston, mainly for use on mineral trains serving the South Yorkshire coalfields.

During the mid-1950s the Western Region, after much deliberation, opted for the return of some Stanier 8Fs, in preference to a batch of new Standard 9F 2-10-0s then under construction. The Western Region, perhaps not surprisingly, since this was a time when many ex-GWR men still hankered after all things Swindon, quite categorically stated, they only wanted machines built in their Wiltshire factory.

By April 1957 30 8Fs had returned to the Western Region. In September 1955 No 48431 renewed its acquaintance with Newton Abbot shed (83A). The next month it was transferred to St Philip's Marsh (82B) in Bristol, where it stayed until the turn of the decade.

Following the 8Fs return to the Western Region the ejectors were moved much nearer to the front of the boiler, which meant the connecting pipe-work could be shortened considerably. Thus the WR batch were easily distinguishable from their LM counterparts, although only on the left hand side!

The early years of the conflict took a heavy toll on the resources of Britain's railways, and the Railway Executive eventually sanctioned further batches of new freight engines, specifically for home use, with the proviso that they were all built to the same design. Following an evaluation of the heavyweight types operated by the 'Big Four' the Stanier 8F was chosen, and from 1943 the workshops of the Great Western, London North Eastern, and Southern Railways, as well as those of the LMS, began constructing locomotives to Stanier's 8F design.

In total 852 8Fs were manufactured, the final one in 1946. In addition to home service, 228 were despatched abroad, mainly to the Middle East. Some sent to Iraq remained at work in the early 1970s, while in Turkey others soldiered on into the 1980s.

British Railways eventually had 666 on its books, although three, Nos 48773-5 were not taken over from the WD until 1957. For the fascinating career of one of this trio, No 48773, now to be found on the Severn Valley Railway, see a companion volume in this series, *Severn Valley Locomotives – As They Were*, pages 58-60).

Along with the 'Black 5s', they became the mainstay of BR steam power in its last year. At the beginning of 1968 150 remained in capital stock, the last examples not being withdrawn until August 1968.

In January 1960 No 48431 became the responsibility of Old Oak Common (81A) shed, before it went back to Bristol in December 1962, this time to the city's ex-Midland shed, Bristol Barrow Road (82E). While maintained in Bristol and London, it was utilised side by side with former GWR 2-8-0s on the usual heavy goods duties, but was noted, very occasionally, on passenger work

Finally, in January 1964, No 48431 was transferred to Bath Green Park (82F), for Somerset & Dorset line duties, only to be withdrawn in May. In August 1964 it was dragged into Woodham's scrapyard at Barry. With that firm concentrating their resources on breaking up redundant BR wagons, the 8F lingered for nearly eight years, except for the removal of various fittings, virtually unscathed.

In May 1972 No 48431 became the 19th engine to be towed away from Barry, destined for a new home on the KWVR, the first step on the long road to an active life again. Six other former BR 8Fs have been preserved, while one has been repatriated from Turkey.

A close-up platform view of No 48431 at Bristol Temple Meads on 6th April 1963, which shows clearly the position of the ejector, as adapted by the Western Region, together with the much shortened pipework. This feature, made the WR Stanier 8Fs readily identifiable from the majority of the class, based on the London Midland Region, which retained the ejector in the original position as seen on page 30. Ken Davies

No 51218

The Lancashire & Yorkshire Railway class 21 was introduced by Aspinall in 1891. It was a short wheel-based 0-4-0ST intended for shunting dock lines and other yards with tight radius curves. Tipping the scales at a mere 21 tons 5 cwt, and with driving wheels of only 3ft 0⅜in diameter, the class proved more than adequate for the purpose.

Horwich Works built 57 class 21s between 1891 and 1910, No 51218 being the first of a batch of 10, constructed in 1901, as L&Y No 68. Over the years it travelled widely and was often located far beyond the old L&Y boundaries.

Little detail is known of its early life, except that the L&Y Locomotive Allocations List of 1921 states the engine was on loan to Goole. It was based there in 1931, then numbered 11218 in the LMS stock list.

Hybrid builder's plate on No 51218. Tom Heavyside

Below: **As Lancashire & Yorkshire Railway No 68 the locomotive is seen at Sandhills, Liverpool, in 1922.** B C Lane collection

Opposite page: **In immaculate condition outside Horwich Works, after some remedial work, No 51218 waits to commence the long journey back to South Wales on 15th June 1963. Note the solid wooden buffers, and the position of the builder's plate on the sandbox.** Tom Heavyside

Thereafter its official shed allocations were as follows:

November	1932	Shrewsbury
November	1939	Preston
November	1940	Edge Hill, Liverpool
April	1941	Birkenhead
September	1941	Preston
July	1942	Edge Hill, Liverpool
March	1943	Shrewsbury
April	1943	Preston
November	1945	Springs Branch, Wigan
August	1946	Preston
October	1950	Monument Lane, Birmingham
December	1950	Crewe South
August	1953	Preston
October	1953	Crewe South
December	1958	Bank Hall, Liverpool
February	1959	Widnes
August	1959	Bristol Barrow Road
December	1962	Swansea East Dock
June	1964	Neath

It was withdrawn in September 1964.

During the 1930s, while it was attached to Shrewsbury shed, it is known to have worked spasmodically at Trench. Also, it had a couple of interesting spells away on loan. First, in 1933, it assisted in building a diversion line to avoid a troublesome tunnel on the ex-North Stafford-shire Railway branch between Tean and Cheadle. Then for nearly three months, from 6th March 1937, it was hired to Barking Power Station in east London, presumably while their own locomotive was out of commission. This was followed by a short stop-over at British Thomson-Houston, Rugby, in July 1937, while returning to Shrewsbury.

On 1st January 1948 the 23 members of the class which passed into BR ownership, were based mainly in former L&Y territory. However, as noted in the previous column, the travels of No 51218 (as it then became) continued under state ownership. Indeed, it ended its BR days as part of Western Region stock.

When first moved to the WR, to Bristol Barrow Road (82E) it was to assist sister engine No 51217 at Radstock, where a very low bridge demanded the use of a diminutive locomotive. This duty finished in 1960.

At the end of 1962 it was despatched to South Wales, intended as a replacement for ex-Powlesland & Mason 0-4-0ST No 1151 at Swansea East Dock (87D). In the event No 51218 failed en route near Port Talbot and was dumped at Duffryn Yard shed (87B), pending a decision as to its future. It was subsequently returned to its birthplace for repair at Horwich Works. After release from Horwich, in June 1963, a second fraught journey back to the Principality meant it was early autumn before it became of any benefit to Swansea.

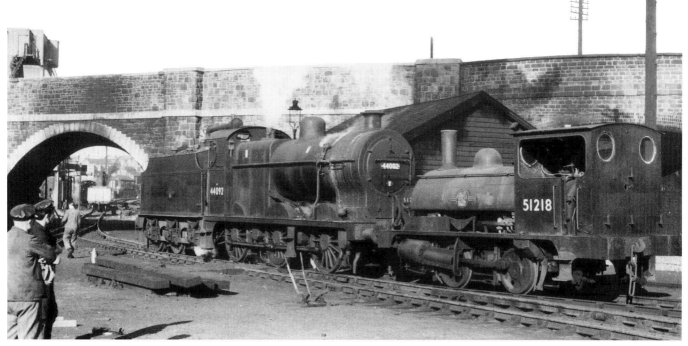

When Swansea East Dock shed closed in June 1964, No 51218 was transferred to Neath (87A), but was stored on arrival. It was withdrawn in September, being the last 'Lanky' locomotive to remain in BR capital stock.

It set foot on Worth Valley metals in January 1965, the first locomotive to arrive at the embryonic KWVR. Even then this was not the end of its roving. After renovation it was used on three brake-van specials from Rochdale to Whitworth on 19th February 1967, and in 1969 was loaned to Brown & Polson, Trafford Park, Manchester, as stand-in for their own locomotive.

In August 1975, it was away again, this time to the 150th anniversary celebrations of the Stockton & Darlington Railway, at Shildon. There, No 51218 deservedly took its place amongst many aristocrats of the steam world, and at the end of the week long event, in the concluding cavalcade procession, it proudly paraded before tens of thousands, who had gathered to pay homage to steams place in railway history. An eventful life indeed for a humble 'Pug' locomotive!

Left: **As local enginemen look on with interest, LMS 4F 0-6-0 No 44092 is commandeered to shunt No 51218 at Bristol Barrow Road shed, on 5th October 1962. No 44092 was on a visit from Saltley shed (21A).** R C Riley

Top right: **Far from its L&Y roots, No 51218 bides time at the back of Bristol Barrow Road shed, together with sister engine No 51217, on 28th May 1961.** Ivo Peters

Right: **After failing near Port Talbot, while being moved from Bristol to Swansea, No 51218 is pictured with its rods dismantled at Duffryn Yard shed, on 12th April 1963, prior to its return to Horwich for attention.** Peter Hutchinson

No 52044

When Barton Wright was appointed Locomotive Superintendent of the Lancashire & Yorkshire Railway in October 1875, his main priority was to design a new 0-6-0 freight engine. The first of his inside-cylindered class 25s were received from Kitson's in July 1876, and by 1887 280 were in service. All but 40, had been ordered from various private locomotive building companies.

In 1889, Aspinall, Barton Wright's successor, introduced a more powerful 0-6-0, the L&Y class 27, with a tractive effort of 21,130lb, against the 17,545lb of the class 25s. Further, Aspinall decided to rebuild all but the last 50 of the Barton Wright engines as 0-6-0STs, the conversions being carried out at Horwich Works. The spare tenders were then coupled to the new class 27s.

Known as 'Ironclads' the future No 52044 was one of the last batch of 50 class 25s, being built by Beyer Peacock, Manchester, in 1887, as their works No 2840. It entered service as L&Y No 957, later becoming LMS No 12044.

In 1921 it was on the books of Goole shed, and was still there at Nationalisation in 1948, along with four others of the class. Though the first had been condemned back in November 1930 a total of 25 'Ironclads' came into BR ownership. They had a power classification of 2F.

From January 1950 No 52044 (its new BR number) was based at Wakefield shed (25A). It was withdrawn from there as the sole survivor of the class in July 1959. It had recorded 1,154,163 miles over the previous 72 years. Following the disposal of its last active sister, No 52016 at Patricroft (10C) in October 1956, No 52044 became quite a celebrity – a foretaste of its life to come! This despite doing very little work in its last two years, it only covered 3,244 miles in 1958 and a mere 45 miles in 1959.

Thankfully, the year 1959 was not the end for the 'Ironclad', the locomotive then being privately purchased from BR, and housed at Retford, until moved to the Worth Valley, in March 1965. Since the release of the celebrated feature film 'The Railway Children', filmed on the KWVR in 1970, the engine, like its Worth Valley companion No 5775, has been oft-seen by a wide audience in its leading role as the 'Green Dragon' locomotive. A far cry from trundling loose-coupled goods wagons around the White Rose County – its regular lot in earlier times.

Below: **No 52044 in its early days at Wakefield shed on 23rd June 1950. Its number is in large LMS style numerals, the first digit of which has been changed from 1 to 5, an economical way of giving the locomotive its new BR identity. The locomotive's BR smokebox numberplate had yet to be affixed at this date.** W A Boyden

Opposite page: **While a friendly crew pose for the camera, No 52044 is viewed against an evocative industrial background, on the ex-L&Y Silkstone branch, near Barnsley, on 11th September 1953.** F W Shuttleworth

No 58926

In 1873, Francis Webb, Chief Mechanical Engineer of the London & North Western Railway introduced a very basic inside-cylindered 0-6-0 class, referred to as 'Coal Engines'. Eight years later, by the simple expedient of adding a trailing axle, coal bunker and side-tanks in place of a tender, an 0-6-2T variant of these was created, engines which became known as 'Coal Tanks'.

The LNWR built 300 'Coal Tanks', but at the time of the Grouping in 1923, numbers had been reduced to 292. They were to be seen in all parts of the old LNWR empire and, while originally intended for shunting and goods work, were often found on local passenger trains. Indeed, some were push-pull fitted for branch line work. They had a tractive effort of 16,530lb.

Now the only survivor of its kind, No 1054 first emerged from Crewe Works in September 1888. From 1923 the LMS identified it as No 7799. In view of subsequent events it seems incredible to relate that it was actually withdrawn in January 1939, but later, due to the increased demands on resources caused by World War Two, was reinstated to traffic in December 1940.

Thus more than fortunate to survive, it was among 64 'Coal Tanks' bequeathed by the LMS to BR in 1948. It lingered on for another ten years as BR No 58926. Like the rest of the class it was never fitted with a smokebox numberplate.

The engine's allocations are known only from 1927 and are listed in the next column. They give a clear indication of the type's widespread use in former LNWR territory.

January	1927	Bangor
October	1930	Abergavenny
February	1936	Shrewsbury
December	1940	Patricroft, Manchester
January	1942	Shrewsbury
May	1946	Warrington
July	1947	Plodder Lane, Bolton
November	1948	Edge Hill, Liverpool
November	1949	Bletchley
September	1950	Shrewsbury
May	1954	Abergavenny
September	1955	Shrewsbury (See page 42)

No 58926 departs from Leighton Buzzard with the 5.38pm service to Dunstable on 17th June 1950. Passenger services on this branch came to an end on 2nd July 1962.
Ken Nunn collection, courtesy of the
Locomotive Club of Great Britain

After a period on loan to the National Coal Board, No 58926 is seen stored with classmate No 58891, at Abercynon shed, on 26th May 1955. At this time both locomotives retained their push-pull gear. Brian Morrison

Published lists show No 58926 as reallocated to Shrewsbury in September 1955 and, even though subsequent issues of the Ian Allan ABC Locoshed Book show the engine as belonging to 84G, it seems doubtful if it ever moved back to Shropshire. There is much contemporary evidence to support this supposition.

In the mid-1950s the engine was loaned to the National Coal Board and saw use at Ynysybwl Colliery, near Pontypridd. On its return to BR it was stored for a time at Abercynon shed (88E), and was next noted at Abergavenny on 3rd October 1955. It is perhaps worth mentioning that in September 1955 Abergavenny became a sub-shed to Pontypool Road (86G).

Over the next two years there were many published sightings of No 58926 at Abergavenny, and it is known to have been steamed spasmodically, particularly in the winter months when put on stand-by for possible snow-plough duties. However recorded mileage for the years 1955 to 1957 totalled only 191.

On 4th January 1958 the Stephenson Locomotive Society appropriately requested the 'Coal Tank' to double-head with class 7F 0-8-0 No 49121, a special to mark the closure of the former LNWR Abergavenny to Merthyr route. The photograph of this occasion, below, shows No 58926 sporting a 84G Shrewsbury shed-plate.

Abergavenny sub-shed closed on 4th January 1958, whereupon No 58926 moved to the parent depot, Pontypool Road. Here it became a shed-mate of its future KWVR companion, ex-GWR 0-6-0PT No 5775 (see pages 6 to 7). That winter it was again kept in steam for snow-clearing activities, being withdrawn in September 1958 and returned to Crewe.

Fortunately the last rites were never pronounced, for the engine was bought by Mr J M Dunn, a former shedmaster at Bangor. After restoration as LNWR No 1054, and a short period of residence at Hednesford, Staffs, it was presented to The National Trust, and given a home in the Industrial Railway Museum, Penrhyn Castle, Llandegai, near Bangor, not far from its home in the late 1920s.

Conditions at Penrhyn Castle were rather cramped, and in 1973 The National Trust loaned the engine to the Dinting Railway Centre. Here it was put back in running-order in time for the 'Rocket 150' celebrations at Rainhill in 1980. Since then No 1054 has enjoyed the occasional outing on BR main lines, and visited other preserved railway sites. With the collapse of the Dinting project in 1990, the KWVR became the permanent home for No 1054 which still remains the property of The National Trust.

No 58926 and class 7F 0-8-0 No 49121 halt at Brynmawr en route from Abergavenny to Merthyr in charge of the SLS special on 4th January 1958 mentioned in the text.
Harold D Bowtell

No 68077

During the early years of World War Two, as the Allied forces made strategic plans for any future invasion of mainland Europe, it soon became apparent that to assist the efficient transportation of materials, a fleet of powerful shunting engines would be required. Basic, sturdy, easy to maintain locomotives, yet ones which would be reliable under the worst possible working conditions were called for.

First thoughts were to build more of the already proven LMS 'Jinty' 0-6-0Ts. However, after much consideration, the Ministry of Supply decided on a new design from Hunslet's, based on some of their recent practice. To record that the finished inside-cylindered 0-6-0ST 'Austerity' class was a resounding success is, in many ways, an understatement.

The prototype left Hunslet's in January 1943, but with the War Department's needs being way beyond the capacity of their Leeds factory, copies of the drawings were handed to other private locomotive builders. Thus, during the war years, examples were also constructed by W G Bagnall, Andrew Barclay, Hudswell Clarke, Robert Stephenson & Hawthorns, and the Vulcan Foundry. In total the MoS ordered 377 'Austerities'.

Following the invasion of Europe in 1944 'Austerities' were shipped to Belgium, France and Holland, and later a few went to West Africa. They did sterling work. Fortunately their wartime exploits were soon at an end, and by 1946, many had become surplus to MoS requirements. Even so, some were destined never to return to British shores, 27 being retained by the Netherlands State Railways, while others entered industrial service in Holland and France.

On the home front redundant 'Austerities' soon became much sought after machines. Numerous examples were snapped up for use in industry, while the London & North Eastern Railway purchased 75, classifying them J94.

Such was the success of this wartime design that production continued, on and off, until March 1964, when the last two were despatched from Hunslet's for work in the National Coal Board's South Yorkshire coalfield. In fact, the NCB were the most prolific users of the type, with over 250 of the 485 eventually built, serving the coal industry at some time or other. It should be mentioned that in 1954, a seventh builder became involved in their construction, when Yorkshire Engine Company supplied eight to United Steel Companies Ltd.

No 68077 was the last of an Army order from Andrew Barclay's, Caledonia Works, Kilmarnock, works No 2215. It was not completed until January 1947. Although allocated the WD number 71466 and painted khaki, it was delivered direct from Barclay's to the LNER as their No 8077. It was put to work at Immingham Docks, one of 25 allocated to Immingham shed.

Under the BR renumbering scheme the prefix 6 was added to the number. In August 1949 it was reliveried plain black, and given an extended bunker, as were most of the BR 'Austerities'. No 68077 remained attached to Immingham shed (40B) until January 1959, when it moved to Hornsey (34B), then Boston (40F) in July 1961, and Colwick (40E) in June 1962. It was withdrawn at the end of 1962.

The engine was then sold to the NCB, South Yorkshire Area, one of six BR J94s which moved on to the coal industry. It was soon put to work

The ungainly features of the Hunslet-designed 'Austerity' 0-6-0STs are apparent in this view of No 68077 at Hornsey shed, on 18th March 1961. Some wag has chalked 'Venus' on the bufferbeam – the name of the ancient Roman goddess of love seems somewhat inappropriate for an 'Austerity'!
Norman Preedy

as NCB No 14 at Orgreave Colliery, Woodhouse, near Sheffield, but with the extended bunker removed. During the autumn of 1968 it was transferred to Maltby Main Colliery near Rotherham, but by the summer of 1970 was out of use. After languishing at Maltby for over a year it was purchased for future service on the KWVR.

As a further testimony to this war-time design, it should be noted, that in all, 70 members of the type have been preserved at sites throughout Britain, while another four are known to be still extant overseas.

No suitable photograph has come to light of No 68077 while employed by the NCB, at Orgreave or Maltby Main Collieries. This picture of Hunslet-built 'Austerity' 0-6-0ST No 3168 of 1944, on its last day of service at Wheldale Colliery, Castleford, on 24th September 1982, is included as a representation of the type of work done by the class for the NCB. Note the conical shaped chimney, a distinguishing feature of those 'Austerities' fitted with a Hunslet under-feed stoker system. Thankfully, although this steaming meant the end of commercial service for the class in the Yorkshire coalfields, there is still a much valued place for the type on Britain's preserved railways. No 3168, like No 68077, is still domiciled in the White Rose County, at the Embsay Steam Railway, near Skipton.
Tom Heavyside

No 75078

In original condition, as outshopped from Swindon Works in January 1956 with a single chimney, No 75078 bides time at Eastleigh shed on 26th March 1960.
Frank Hornby

Under the direction of R A Riddles, Swindon Works built 80 BR Standard class 4 4-6-0s for mixed traffic purposes. The first, No 75000 appeared in May 1951 and incorporated the, by-then, usual modern aids for ease of maintenance, such as a self-emptying ashpan, rocking grate, and self-cleaning smokebox. A maximum axle load of only 17 tons 5 cwt gave them a wide route availability.

No 75078 left Swindon in January 1956, one of a batch of 15 for the Southern Region, constructed before the series 75050-64 destined for the London Midland Region, the last of which, No 75064 took to the rails in June 1957. These 30, including No 75078, were coupled to high-sided BR1B tenders, which could carry 7 tons of coal and 4,725 gallons of water. The cut-away

version attached to the earlier members of the class held 6 tons and 3,500 gallons.

Initially Nos 75070-79 went to Exmouth Junction shed (72A), but their stay in the West Country was brief, for in May 1956 they were all moved away. Nos 75075-79 were transferred to the small shed at Basingstoke (70D). In fact, No 75078 was to spend all its BR days working from Southern Region, western section depots.

In late 1957 Swindon fitted a double blast-pipe and chimney to No 75029. This gave a marked increase in steaming capacity, even with poor quality coal. Later the Southern Region decided to capitalise on this improvement by carrying out similar modifications to its 75xxxs, No 75078 having a double-chimney fitted during a general overhaul at Eastleigh Works in October 1961.

No 75078 remained a Basingstoke engine until March 1963, whereupon it was transferred to Nine Elms (70A), the main shed serving Waterloo station in London. It continued to be seen quite often at Basingstoke, while working semi-fasts on the Bournemouth and Salisbury main lines, as well as some freight and parcels duties.

In May 1965 No 75078 moved to Eastleigh, (70D). This code had previously been that of Basingstoke shed which lost its allocation of locomotives in September 1963, although the site was retained for stabling locomotives and as a crew signing-on point. Its sphere of operation while at Eastleigh continued more or less as before, but in July 1966, with the need for steam

locomotives rapidly diminishing, BR decided to withdraw No 75078 from the active list. Some of its Southern sisters remained on duty until July 1967, when steam finished on the routes out of Waterloo, while a few members of the class on the LMR, based in the North West, continued to work into the summer of 1968.

For No 75078 it was then assumed only one more journey remained, that to the breakers' yard. In November 1966 it was delivered to Woodham Bros, Barry, South Wales, where it languished for 5½ years.

During the early 1970s, as the burgeoning preservation movement looked for additional power, modern, versatile engines, such as No 75078, not surprisingly, became prime candi-

dates for rescue bids. With the necessary payment made, No 75078 left Barry in June 1972 to take up permanent residence on the KWVR. Five other members of the class are still in existence, including three rescued from Woodham's scrapyard.

No 75078 slows for the Chilcompton stop, while heading a Templecombe to Bath local train, along the erstwhile Somerset & Dorset Railway in October 1962. Derek Cross

Right: **Now fitted with a double-chimney, No 75078 is seen at Nine Elms shed, during a visit to the capital, on 7th October 1962.** Peter Hutchinson

Below: **Here No 75078, in charge of the seven-coach 15.35 London Waterloo to Bournemouth service, heads through the New Forest, west of Brockenhurst, on 23rd June 1966. The engine was withdrawn by BR the following month.** Peter Hutchinson

No 78022

The BR Standard class 2 Moguls were basically a continuation, with some detail differences, of the LMS taper-boilered 2-6-0s introduced by Ivatt in 1946. The original Ivatt design had already proved itself, production continuing until 1953, by which time 128 were in traffic numbered 46400-527.

BR ordered 65 Standard class 2s, and they emerged from Darlington Works between 1952 and 1956 as Nos 78000-64. Every Region, except the Southern, had an initial allocation and, like their Ivatt forebears, soon demonstrated themselves as ideal workhorses on secondary duties.

No 78022 was part of a London Midland Region consignment of 35 engines. It went straight to Millhouses shed (19B) in May 1954, but became part of Eastern Region stock in February 1958, when Millhouses was recoded 41C under some wholesale regional boundary changes.

Under ER control the engine continued to work local passenger services in the Sheffield area until January 1962. After this, for a short time, it rubbed shoulders with some of the aristocrats of Eastern Region motive power, while based at Doncaster (36A). Thereafter, from the beginning of August 1962, followed six weeks in the capital, at the ex-Great Eastern Railway Stratford shed (30A), then three months in the Fen Country at March (31B). At the latter shed most of its time was spent in store.

With little prospect of any further work on the Eastern Region, No 78022 was transferred back to London Midland hands in early December 1962, going first to the Furness outpost of Barrow (12E). It moved to Merseyside in May 1963, based at Aintree (27B), and finally, at the end of the year, to Lostock Hall (10D). While at 10D it could often be seen ambling along on local freight trips and, on other occasions, as Preston station pilot engine. It was condemned in September 1966, after just over 12 years service, albeit in rather varied surroundings!

Fortunately, as events turned out, the tender for the engine from Woodham Bros was accepted by BR. In March 1967 No 78022 made the long sad journey to South Wales. It stood forlorn and neglected, but not forgotten, for eight years, in what became perhaps the most well-known scrapyard in the world, along with three other members of the class.

Above: **A well-groomed No 78022 shunts vigorously at the south end of Preston station, while on station pilot duty, on 30th May 1964.** Peter J Fitton

Opposite page: **No 78022 draws a Sheffield to Leeds stopping train into Royston station on 8th August 1960.** David Idle

No 78022 was rescued from Barry for future service on the KWVR in June 1975, the 67th engine removed from the yard by preservationists. It was steamed for the first time at Haworth in 1993 after a long overhaul.

In early 1995 it was controversially fitted with a Giesl ejector, similar to that on No 34092, which gives it a far different front-end appearance. Future trials will determine if the system enhances steaming capacity, as has proved the case with so many other classes in the past.

It is pleasing to note that the other three BR Standard class 2 Moguls purchased by Woodhams, in the 1960s, have also been saved for posterity.

No 80002

The BR Standard class 4 2-6-4 tanks were designed at Brighton Works. Originally they were intended to be modelled on the successful LMS Fairburn class 4 2-6-4Ts built from 1945, but with standard fittings. In the event some quite major alterations were made in order to give the class a much wider route availability.

The first Standard class 4 2-6-4T constructed, No 80010, left Brighton Works in July 1951, for work on the Southern Region. In all 155 were built over five years, 10 at Doncaster, 15 at Derby, and the remainder at Brighton. These very pleasing locomotives subsequently ranged far and wide, throughout the BR network.

No 80002 was part of the first Lot of 10 ordered from Derby Works for the Scottish Region. By the time it appeared in October 1952, numerous Brighton-built examples were already at work. It was despatched north to Motherwell shed (66B), moving on to Polmadie (66A) the next month.

Below: **During the period it was shedded at Beattock, in April 1963, No 80002 lends a hand to an unidentified Stanier class 5 4-6-0, lifting a very mixed assortment of stock up the unrelenting 10-mile Beattock bank, on the ex-Caledonian Railway main line from Carlisle to Glasgow Central. The train straddles Harthope Viaduct, under which the original path of the main A74 road (now upgraded to motorway status) can be seen passing between the far columns.**
Derek Cross

During the 1950s the class became very familiar around Glasgow. In 1959, 20 were on the books of Polmadie, with a further 9 at Corkerhill (67A). They regularly had charge of many of the suburban passenger trains in and out of the city's Central and St Enoch stations.

After giving sterling service around the commercial centre of Scotland, for almost a decade, No 80002 was transferred south, along with its sister No 80001, to Beattock (68D), in June 1962. The work allocation on the roster board at this small shed, situated in the comparative tranquillity of the Lowther hills, was very different from the hustle and bustle encountered at the massive Polmadie depot, although, in some ways, every bit as taxing. Engines allocated to 68D were required to bank heavy trains up the ferocious 10-mile Beattock incline, where sustained all out effort was required on gradients as steep as 1 in 74. Occasional respite came when called upon to haul the local trip freight along the former Caledonian Railway line to Moffat .

The Moffat branch, which had lost its passenger services as long ago as December 1954, closed completely in April 1964 and that month No 80002 returned to its old stamping grounds, again based at Polmadie. It remained there until it retired from active service in March 1967.

An ignominious end in a scrapyard, the fate of the rest of the Scottish-allocated Standard 4MT tanks, was staved off for No 80002, by a move to Cowlairs sidings, Glasgow, for use as a stationary boiler for carriage heating purposes. The job didn't last long, following which, in 1969, it was moved south to the Worth Valley. Altogether 15 members of this attractive and successful class have been preserved.

Opposite top: **On this occasion (date unknown) little exertion is needed by No 80002, as it ambles away from Beattock, down the branch towards Moffat. The main line north to Glasgow passes through the right hand arch of the bridge in the background.**
T G Hepburn / Rail Archive Stephenson

Opposite bottom: **Shortly after its return to Polmadie shed from Beattock, No 80002 runs into Inverkip station, with the 11.30am Wemyss Bay to Glasgow Central service on 30th June 1964.**
Hamish Stevenson

Right: **On 18th December 1965 a grimy No 80002 darkens the sky at Bogston, with a train from Gourock to Glasgow Central. A distinguished visitor to Clydeside, seen on the right, is the liner *Queen Elizabeth*.** Hamish Stevenson

Below: **No 80002 departs from the island platform at Upper Greenock, then working a Wemyss Bay to Glasgow Central service, on 30th June 1964.** Hamish Stevenson

D226 *Vulcan*

During the 1950s, influenced by British Railways increasing interest in internal combustion engines, as were railways overseas, many private locomotive builders began to realise that their long term future could hinge on their successful diversification into this field.

Thus, in 1956, English Electric, then the owners of the Vulcan Foundry at Newton-le-Willows, Lancashire, constructed two identical 500hp 0-6-0 diesels, one with electric and the other with hydraulic transmission systems. Both were made available to BR for evaluation purposes.

For three years D226 (works No 2345), the diesel-electric version, and the hydraulic example D227, were used extensively by BR.

They undertook yard shunting, and transfer freight work, in places as far apart as Liverpool, Doncaster, Stratford and Bristol. They were also tried as bankers on the Gunhouse incline, near Scunthorpe, for two weeks, at the end of which the local men were glad to see them move on, the engines not having sufficient power for such arduous work.

In many ways the locomotives fell between two stools. They had more power than was normally needed for shunting work, yet they were not really versatile enough for general duties on the main line. In consequence the design was not perpetuated, although the diesel-electric version proved the superior of the two.

Towards the end of their BR wanderings, they were officially renumbered D0226 and D0227, to prevent a clash with the new English Electric Type 4s, later class 40s, then being introduced. At the conclusion of the trial period both locomotives were returned to Vulcan.

Regrettably D227 was scrapped, but D226 remained at Vulcan until March 1966, where it was started-up occasionally for internal duties.

It was then made available to the emergent KWVR and shortly afterwards named *Vulcan*. It has since proved a valued asset, particularly for works and shunting duties, as well as for emergency use on the service trains.

Above: **D226 at Speke Junction, Liverpool, in charge of a local trip freight on 1st December 1958.** J A Peden

Below: **During its time in London D226 is seen outside Stratford shed, on 5th July 1959.** J F Davies/Photomatic-Rail Archive Stephenson

D2511

By the dawn of the 1960s BR had opted for what later became classes 03 and 08 as its standard designs for shunting work. Despite this, shunting locomotives to some new specifications continued to be ordered, and during 1961-62 BR took delivery of ten 204hp 0-6-0 diesel-mechanical locomotives from Hudswell Clarke of Leeds.

Power was provided by a Gardner 8L3 engine, as used in the class 03s, but they were able to generate a higher tractive effort of 19,245lb, as opposed to the 15,300lb of the latter. Aesthetically they were much improved over previous Hudswell Clarke engines and were devoid of the steam-type chimney often fitted by that company.

Seven of the ten, including D2511, works D1202 of 1961, were allocated to Barrow (12E – later recoded 12C) and used extensively around the docks there. D2511 had its future KWVR

companion No 78022 for company for five months from December 1962. In October 1966 it became parted from her sisters when moved north, along the coast, to Workington (12D).

As non-standard the class were all withdrawn in 1967, D2511 going in December of that year. They never received a TOPS number and remained in the standard green livery of the period.

During the late 1960s the National Coal Board were on the look-out for suitable second-hand diesel locomotives, to replace their ageing steam fleet. Four of the class were acquired by the NCB, three for the Doncaster Area, and one for the South Yorkshire Area. D2511, one of the fortunate quartet, renumbered as NCB BRM5477, worked at Brodsworth Colliery, near Doncaster, from May 1968. Collision damage in 1977 precipitated its withdrawal.

Its future was quickly secured by private purchase and the engine arrived on the Worth Valley during the autumn of 1977. It is the only one of its type still extant.

D2511 at Derby Works on 2nd October 1966, before its move to Workington later that month. Frank Hornby

D3336

In October 1952 British Railways introduced an 0-6-0 350hp diesel-electric shunting locomotive No 13000. Powered by a 6-cylinder English Electric 6KT engine, later uprated to 400hp, it was to prove a major success story.

The design was the culmination of some 20 years work by the 'Big Four' companies and the private locomotive building industry, English Electric having a major input into developments throughout this period. Between 1952 and 1962 1193 of these machines were produced, although some had Crossley or Blackstone engines and different transmission systems. Only the EE version has been retained by BR in recent times, the others being withdrawn as non-standard.

Later classified 08, the type has handled the vast majority of BR's shunting requirements since the mid-1960s, except on lines where a lighter axle-weight or shorter wheel-based locomotive was a necessity. While in recent years their ranks have been thinned considerably, due to changing operational requirements, they are still a common sight throughout the main line system.

Many of the locomotives were far from life expired when withdrawn, and some have been purchased by private industrial users. The preservation world quickly realised the worth of these functional, if somewhat characterless locomotives, and over 30 can now be found dotted around Britain, enjoying a new lease of life at various sites run by railway preservationists.

The KWVR took delivery of Darlington manufactured No 13336 in November 1985. When new in February 1957 it was the last to be turned out in black livery, before the introduction of the standard green colour scheme for diesel locomotives on BR. The number was soon amended to D3336, then altered to 08 266 under the TOPS renumbering scheme. In later years it sported the BR corporate blue identity.

Its first three months were spent at Sheffield's Darnall shed (41A) before a move to King's Cross (34A) in May 1957. Eleven months later it was back at Darnall, transferring to the new Tinsley depot when this opened in May 1964. It spent its last four years in BR ownership, from August 1981, at Shirebrook in the east Midlands, before being rescued from the Swindon scrap-line, for use on the KWVR.

Left: **Sandwiched between two sister locos, and before the first digit of the number was amended from 1 to D, No 13336 rests at Staveley (GC) shed (41H), near Chesterfield, on 19th April 1959. The locomotives have plain ends – the yellow and black wasp warning stripes had yet to be introduced.** Industrial Railway Society / Brian Webb collection

Above: **Painted in BR blue livery and with the yellow and black warning stripes very prominent, as 08 266, our locomotive is seen at Wath depot on 29th March 1980. Note that as well as bearing its TOPS number, the BR double-arrow insignia has replaced the earlier BR roundel emblem on the body panel, as seen in the earlier photograph.** Norman Preedy

D5209

The BR Derby-designed Type 2 Bo-Bo diesel-electric locomotives were a direct result of the 1955 BR Modernisation Plan. Only 20 were ordered at first, the prototype D5000, fitted with a Sulzer 1,160hp engine, being ready for inspection in July 1958.

In its hasty and headlong rush to be rid of steam, BR was soon proliferating some of the early diesel designs, even before there had been time for proper evaluation. However, the faith shown in these Type 2s was fully justified, and frames for the class continued to be cut until 1967. Those produced from April 1961 housed an uprated Sulzer 1,250hp engine.

All told 478 were built, the bulk in BR's own workshops at Crewe, Darlington and Derby, with 36 coming from Beyer Peacock's Gorton Foundry, Manchester, during 1965-66. 151 carried the 1,160hp engine and 327 the more powerful version. In later life they became classes 24

and 25 respectively. Over the years they could be seen at work on most parts of the BR network on both passenger and goods duties.

D5209 was built at Derby Works in June 1963, and as such has a Sulzer 1,250hp engine. Its depot allocations, ranging across the London Midland, Scottish, and Western Regions, are indicative of the type's widespread use. These were as follows:

June	1963	Toton
July	1963	Cricklewood
February	1968	Longsight, Manchester
March	1968	Carlisle Kingmoor
June	1968	Preston Division
November	1968	Liverpool Division
November	1970	Manchester Division
January	1972	Newport, Ebbw Junction
July	1972	Bristol Bath Road
May	1974	Cardiff Canton
October	1974	Bristol Bath Road
May	1976	Crewe Diesel Depot (1 week)
May	1976	Haymarket, Edinburgh
May	1978	Eastfield, Glasgow
January	1980	Haymarket, Edinburgh
September	1982	Springs Branch, Wigan
October	1982	Crewe Diesel Depot

The locomotive was renumbered 25 059 in January 1974. It was one of the last few in service in March 1987, when the class became extinct on BR. It was then moved to Vic Berry's yard at Leicester, the graveyard of many class 25s in the 1980s, but was rescued for the KWVR the following October. In total 19 class 25s have been preserved along with four of the less powerful class 24s.

During its first year of service D5209 is buffered-up to an unidentified Stanier 'Jubilee' class 4-6-0, along with sister locomotive D5233 (later No 25 083) in Leeds Holbeck (55A) shed yard, on 10th May 1964. D5233 has a later style body shell – the differences in the position of the grilles being clearly discernible. Gavin Morrison

Left: **Against a backdrop of terraced houses, and with a uniform rake of ICI Procor tanks behind, No 25 059 approaches Northwich station from the west, along former Cheshire Lines Committee tracks, on 18th October 1982. Near the rear of the train can be seen the connection to the ex-LNWR line from Northwich to Sandbach and Crewe.** Tom Heavyside

Below: **Utilised during a Sunday engineering possession of the ex-Highland Railway main line, between Perth and Inverness, No 25 059 ticks-over in the sidings adjacent to Blair Atholl station, on 3rd October 1982. The number was then positioned on the bodyside, rather than below the cab window, while the indicator blinds have been replaced by marker lights. A few days later the locomotive returned to England.** Roger Siviter

Opposite page: **Here No 25 059 returns from Fiddlers Ferry Power Station with some empty merry go round coal wagons at Warrington Arpley, on 4th September 1985. The back of the train is still threading the passageway beneath Warrington Bank Quay station on the electrified West Coast main line, while an alert Arpley signalman has already replaced the home signal to the stop position.** Gavin Morrison

D8031

English Electric's Vulcan Works, Newton-le-Willows, Lancashire, produced the first diesel-electric locomotive for BR following publication of the 1955 Modernisation Plan. No 8000 was released from Vulcan in July 1957. It had a single cab, a Bo-Bo wheel arrangement, and was powered by an EE 8-cylinder 1,000hp engine.

The first batch of 20 were in service by March 1958, working from Devons Road shed in London. Contracts were soon exchanged with EE for further orders. By August 1962 128 had been delivered, 93 from the former Robert Stephenson & Hawthorns factory in Darlington, then owned by English Electric, and the rest by Vulcan. Between 1966 and 1968 Vulcan manufactured a further 100. Numerically they were by far the largest class in the 'Type 1' power classification and, indeed, the most successful.

Based mainly east of the Pennines and in Scotland, the lack of train heating equipment normally prevented their use on passenger services, except in high summer or in an emergency. While in their early years they were employed chiefly on general goods diagrams, latterly, as class 20s, heavy haulage of coal and steel trains, became their more usual forte. They often worked in multiple, coupled nose to nose which, as well as doubling the available power output, obviated the sighting difficulties for the engine crew when working bonnet first.

D8031 was built at the EE Darlington works in late 1959, entering traffic in January 1960. It has two works numbers, EE 2753 and RSH 8063. The early years of its life were spent in Scotland, travelling some of the most scenic lines in Britain, before a permanent move to England occurred in June 1968. In January 1974 it received its TOPS No 20 031.

Its shed allocations are as listed below:

January	1960	Kittybrewster, Aberdeen
October	1965	Inverness
November	1966	Polmadie, Glasgow
September	1967	Haymarket, Edinburgh
June	1968	Nottingham Division
September	1968	Stratford, London
October	1969	York
June	1970	Gateshead
October	1970	Immingham
July	1980	Tinsley, Sheffield
July	1987	Immingham
November	1989	Toton

The engine was first withdrawn by BR in September 1989, only to be reinstated the following November at Toton. It was declared surplus to requirements in September 1990. Purchased by a private consortium for the KWVR, it arrived at Haworth in August 1992, after a trip to MC Metals in Glasgow for asbestos removal.

Although BR have dispensed with the class, over 40 are still in existence, many preserved, including the pioneer D8000 at the National Railway Museum in York. Hunslet-Barclay, Kilmarnock, own a small fleet, often seen on weed-killing trains on the national network. A few have found work in France. Comprehensive coverage of the type and in particular the many and varied liveries they carried is provided in Midland Publishing's book, *Class 20s in Colour*.

Above: **An immaculate No 20031, in the BR corporate blue livery, after overhaul at Derby Works, in August 1977.** Geoff Dowling

Opposite page bottom: **On 1st April 1967 D8031 runs by Carlisle Upperby shed with a load of limestone hoppers from Hardendale Quarry, Shap, heading for Kingmoor Yard. The engine is in green livery, while the yellow warning panel, albeit looking rather grimy, only covers the bottom half of the bonnet. A sign of the times is the batch of steam locomotives seen dead on the shed, a 'Britannia' Pacific being the most prominent.** Derek Cross

Right: **No 20 031 saunters along the four-track section of line at Colton, south of York, with only a brake-van in tow, on 29th July 1982.** John Fozard

Below: **The shirt-sleeved driver of No 20 031 keeps a watchful eye on the line ahead, as he guides his train of empties southbound towards Doncaster station platforms, on the warm sunny morning of 7th July 1977.** Gavin Morrison

M50928 & M51565

A recent acquisition for the KWVR, which arrived in March 1992, is a Derby 'lightweight', class 108 diesel multiple unit consisting of vehicle numbers M50928 and M51565. They were purchased for the railway by Bradford City Council in recognition of the 125th anniversary of the opening of the branch.

Both railcars were built at Derby Carriage & Wagon Works in 1959, and are powered by two Leyland 6-cylinder 150hp engines slung horizontally beneath the chassis. The class were part of BR's drive to modernise local and branch line services in the late 1950s and, indeed, similar vehicles worked on the Worth Valley branch during the 18 months prior to its closure in December 1961.

M51565 is a Motor Composite vehicle, originally having 12 first and 52 second class seats. M50928 is a Motor Brake Second with only 52 seats. No 50928 was renumbered 53928 in 1983, by which time the M prefix, denoting regional allocation, had been dropped. When new they were painted green, but for much of their later life were adorned in BR corporate blue livery.

During their BR days, often coupled to other units, they were variously allocated to Allerton (Liverpool), Buxton, Chester and Newton Heath (Manchester). Finally both moved to Landore shed at Swansea where they were coupled together to form Set No S948. Here regular duties included the highly scenic Central Wales line to Shrewsbury.

No 51565, at a time when attached to unit No 53925, leads the 17.19 Preston to Ormskirk service into Rufford station on 10th June 1985. The driver had previously slowed to a walking pace so as to exchange the appropriate single-line tokens with the signalman. A few moments earlier the latter had operated the manual level-crossing gates at this pleasant rural location.
Tom Heavyside

E79962 & E79964

The costs of operating branch lines in sparsely populated areas had long been a concern of British Railways, as well as its predecessors. Following recommendations made in the 1955 Modernisation Plan, BR decided to experiment with a few 4-wheeled railbuses, although it was 1957 before any orders were placed.

Four British companies, and one from overseas, Waggon & Maschinenbau, Donauworth, West Germany, were awarded contracts. In all 22 were constructed, the first from each company being accepted in 1958.

The two on the KWVR, E79962 and E79964, were among a batch of five, delivered in 1958, from the German builders. They followed closely a well-tried design in use on the Deutsche Bundesbahn. Outshopped in Mala-chite green paint and powered by a Buessing 6-cylinder 150hp engine, they could seat 56 passengers and weighed only 15 tons.

From new the five W&M railbuses worked various branches in East Anglia, including those to Braintree, Maldon, Mildenhall and Saffron Walden. Problems were encountered in obtaining spare parts for the Buessing engines and, in the 1960s, three, including E79964, had these replaced by AEC 150hp 6-cylinder engines.

Despite the introduction of the railbuses, closure of many branch lines could not be prevented. As a consequence, in 1964, the class was placed in store at Cambridge, the two still retaining the original Buessing engines, never to run again on BR.

Later, for a brief period E79964, in company with one of its sisters, ran on the ex-North Eastern Railway Haltwhistle to Alston branch, before being moved south to Buxton in July 1966. Here they replaced two Park Royal-built railbuses on the former Midland Railway line to Miller's Dale. The E prefix to the number was then replaced by M, denoting it to be a London Midland Region vehicle. They became redundant when the Miller's Dale service ceased on 6th March 1967.

No E79964 then moved to Haworth, where No E79962 joined it from store in Cambridge. The former now has a former London Transport bus engine in place of its AEC type. Two further members of the class have been preserved on the North Norfolk Railway at Sheringham.

A portrait of E79962 at Stratford shed in 1959. Martin Welch

Above: **One of the five E7996x series W&M railbuses, based in East Anglia, waits at Witham, prior to leaving with the 3.42pm service along the six-mile ex-Great Eastern Railway branch to Braintree, on 21st March 1959. This line is now electrified.**
Michael Mensing

Opposite page: **M79964 leaves Buxton with a train destined for Miller's Dale on 3rd November 1966. A large yellow warning panel on the front of the unit has replaced the 'cats whiskers' warning stripes which can be seen on the photograph above.**
Martin Welch

Bellerophon

Bellerophon is the senior citizen of the Worth Valley fleet, being built in 1874 by Richard Evans & Co Ltd, for their Haydock Collieries complex in Lancashire, a vast concern intent on being self-reliant for its ancillary needs. They constructed six 0-6-0 well tanks between 1869 and 1887.

Designed by Josiah Evans, son of Richard, they were based on a couple of 0-4-0WTs bought from James Cross & Co of St Helens, in 1866 and 1868. The innovative Evans fitted piston valves to the outside cylinders, 20 years before being used with any success elsewhere.

Bellerophon was the third of the sextet, and was at first identified by the letter 'C'. It was the first to have a Gooch/Stephenson type link motion, the previous two having the Stephenson version. Later the engines were given numbers, *Bellerophon* becoming No 3.

Evans, in addition to owning a quite extensive railway system, enjoyed considerable running powers over adjoining main lines. Thus the engines could often be seen hauling coal along the neighbouring London & North Western Railway between sidings owned by the colliery company, as well as on daily runs to Northwich and back. Further, they were used on the Company's annual works outings to Blackpool, *Bellerophon* being a regular participant.

Bellerophon in seemingly good external condition, at NCB Haydock, on 6th May 1956. Industrial Railway Society/Bernard Mettam collection

The Haydock Collieries, along with their locomotives, were taken over by the National Coal Board, on 1st January 1947. *Bellerophon* was the last of the Evans engines to remain at work, being employed until l964. It was then very kindly donated to the KWVR where it arrived in November 1966.

Now in the care of the Vintage Carriages Trust, based at Ingrow, on the KWVR, it has also been very well received on visits to numerous other preserved lines, and steam centres, since its restoration in 1985.

Below: **By the time of this photograph, taken at Lea Green Colliery, St Helens, on 9th April 1959, *Bellerophon* had been very clearly identified as to its ownership, by the letters NCB along the boiler. Further clarification of ownership can be gleaned from the roundel on the side of the bunker, which reads 'National Coal Board, St Helens, NW Division'.** J F Davies/ Rail Archive Stephenson

No 19

This locomotive is the second ex-Lancashire & Yorkshire Railway class 21 0-4-0ST 'Pug' in preservation – see pages 34 to 37. Based on the KWVR from 1967 to 1990, it is presently on loan to the Southport Railway Centre. It is dealt with in this volume because of its normal affiliation with the KWVR, along with the other engines entrusted to the L&Y Railway Preservation Society (formerly the L&Y Saddletanks Fund).

One of the last batch of 20 of the class built at Horwich in 1910, it first ran as L&Y No 19. In 1921 it was on the books of Newton Heath shed in Manchester. It became LMS No 11243 following the Grouping in 1923. During the 1930s the LMS had a surplus of small shunting locomotives and nine ex-L&Y 'Pugs' were sold to private industry. No 11243 was the first to change hands, bought by John Mowlem in September 1931. With the name *Bassett* painted on the saddletank, it assisted in the construction of the *King George V* dock at Southampton.

In 1933 it was bought by the contractors George Cohen & Sons Ltd. Two years later it was resold to United Glass Bottle Manufacturers Ltd, whereupon it shunted their Charlton, London, headquarters for some 30 years. For most of its time at Charlton it bore the name *Prince*, again painted on the saddletank.

When *Prince's* working days at Charlton were over it was initially saved from an ignominious end in a scrapyard, in January 1967, by a member of the London Railway Preservation Society, and moved to Luton. In November of that year, it returned north, to Worth Valley metals, not far from its original routes, where it was restored to its L&Y appearance. Its present abode, at Southport, is in former 'Lanky' territory.

Right: **During the early 1930s the former L&Y 'Pug', then named *Bassett*, is seen on the Southampton Docks contract in the service of John Mowlem. A home-made wooden weatherboard has been fitted to the side of the cab, to give the crew a little more protection from the elements.** Frank Jones

Above: **No 19 at Sandhills shed (later known as Bank Hall), Liverpool, in company with classmate No 2 in L&Y days. No 2, like No 19, was built at Horwich in 1910. It became** LMS No 11238 after the Grouping, and was withdrawn in July 1931. Regretably, no buyer came forward for No 2, and it was subsequently scrapped. B C Lane collection

No 31 *Hamburg*

The Manchester Ship Canal, opened in 1894, can be ascribed as one of the finest engineering feats of the latter part of the Victorian era. It was built to accommodate some of the largest vessels, and effectively linked the heart of inland Manchester with the ocean highways.

In its heyday millions of tons of cargo, of every description, were moved along its length each year. To serve the docks, as well as the adjacent warehouses and factories, a complex railway network was developed. At its zenith the MSC owned over 230 miles of track.

On opening the MSC retained many of the locomotives used during its construction, but continuing growth of business meant that they soon had to start looking for additional engines.

They first liaised with Peckett's, and then Hunslet's, to supply their needs, but in 1902 they bought an inside-cylindered 0-6-0T, with flangeless centre wheels, from Hudswell Clarke.

The design was destined to become the MSC standard shunter. Indeed, they were a common sight along the canal banks, and on the tracks by the roadsides running through the Trafford Park industrial estate, for over half-a-century.

MSC No 31, was put together by Hudswell Clarke in 1903, works No 679, and named *Hamburg*. The name was removed in 1914, in the general anti-German hysteria of the period which led to the Royal family, as well as this tank engine having to change its name. The engine remained anonymous until 1972.

No 31 was known to MSC staff as a 'short tank', as opposed to similar engines constructed later by Hudswell Clarke's with extended side tanks. The latter were referred to as 'long tanks', these having an increased water capacity of 840 gallons, as against the 580 gallons of the earlier engines. The Hudswell Clarke catalogue described them as the 'Canal' and 'Sweden' classes respectively, the MSC buying 25 of the former and 22 of the latter, the last as late as 1927.

While the last MSC steam duty was undertaken by 'long tank' No 67 on 30th June 1966 (itself based on the KWVR for many years prior to its move to the Middleton Railway in Leeds), the honour of being present at an official ceremony, to mark the changeover from steam to diesel traction, on 6th July 1966 went to No 31, accompanied by sister 'short tank' No 32. A year later No 31 moved to the Worth Valley, while No 32 now normally resides on the East Lancashire Railway, although presently it is disguised as a very effective 'Thomas the Tank Engine' lookalike.

A fine portrait of No 31 at Mode Wheel, on the Manchester Ship Canal railway on a sunny 6th August 1961.
Industrial Railway Society / K J Cooper collection

No 63 *Corby*

Starting in 1881, the rich ironstone deposits around Corby in Northamptonshire, were extracted for almost a century. The establishment of an ironworks at Corby in 1910, later part of the British Steel empire, meant that thereafter, in the main, the ore was processed locally.

Over the years, as the works grew in importance, the quarrying of ore increased commensurately. So much so that at the beginning of the 1950s, the already quite extensive railway system, was expanded even further. This then took in Harringworth, and other quarries, to the north of the town, and obviated the need to rely on BR for the movement of some ore.

The new line, except for one short stretch, was double track. Operations were controlled centrally by colour-light signals. To operate the 'main line', Stewarts & Lloyds, the then owners of Corby, ordered, to their own specifications, from Robert Stephenson & Hawthorns, seven large inside-cylindered 0-6-0STs. Similar in outline to the Hunslet 'Austerity' class, except for a shorter saddletank, they were, in fact, even more powerful. Known as the 56 class, these seven, all built in 1950, were numbered 56 to 62. In later years two more were received from RSH, No 63 in 1954, and No 64 in 1958.

Steam operations at Corby came to a sudden end on 11th January 1969, with the bulk purchase of 23 redundant 650hp Swindon-built D95xx 0-6-0 diesel-hydraulics from BR which were then less than six years old. Five of the class 56s were saved, with three, Nos 57, 62 and 63 arriving on the KWVR later in 1969. They were soon dubbed the 'Uglies' by Worth Valley enginemen. Since then Nos 57 and 62 have moved elsewhere, while No 63 (works No 7761) appropriately carries the name *Corby*.

Above: **The impressive eight-road Pen Green shed at Corby, viewed on 14th September 1965. Four of the nine class 56s at Corby can be seen, including the first of the type No 56 on the far left. No 63, half hidden, is in the centre, while on the right are Nos 57 and** 62, two members of the class that were one time based on the KWVR. No 57 is now at a private location in Shropshire, while No 62 is on the stock list of the Bodmin & Wenford Railway in Cornwall. Hugh Ballantyne

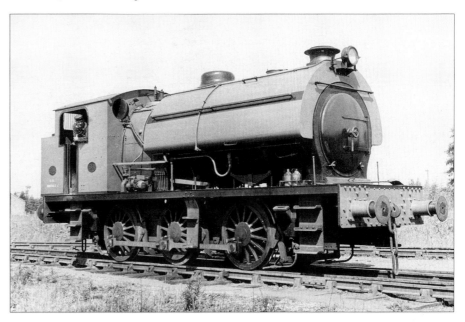

Right: **A very agreeable portrait of No 63 at Pen Green shed, Corby, on a date unknown.** Industrial Railway Society / K J Cooper collection

No 85

Prior to its absorption by the Great Western Railway in 1923, the Taff Vale Railway was one of the major players in South Wales. Its main source of income was the transportation of coal from the Valleys, much of it to the docks located on the Bristol Channel, at Cardiff and Penarth.

In South Wales, distances covered were usually relatively short, the longest journey on the Taff Vale being only 26 miles long. However due to the nature of the terrain, many lines presented operating difficulties in the form of steep inclines and sharp curves. These could be found on both the main lines and the connections off these, to the various collieries.

From their introduction to South Wales during the mid-1880s, locomotives of the 0-6-2T type proved very suitable for these difficult routes. Indeed, the type dominated the haulage of coal traffic in the Valleys until they were usurped by English Electric Type 3s (later class 37s) in the 1960s.

In 1923, the Great Western gained 274 steam locomotives from the Taff Vale. Two hundred and nine of these were 0-6-2Ts of various classes. Among these were nine O2 class engines, built by Neilson Reid & Co of Glasgow, in 1899.

Following the takeover, the GWR continued its established standardisation policies. While some of the engines it inherited were 'Swindonised', others were quickly withdrawn, a fate which befell the Taff Vale O2s during the mid-1920s.

However, for one O2, after 28 years slogging along the Valley lines with rakes of coal wagons in tow, interspersed with the occasional passenger train, a new life beckoned. Withdrawn in January 1927, and after standing idle on the Swindon dump for over two years, GWR No 426, the former Taff Vale No 85 (Neilson Reid works No 5408), was purchased by the Lambton Hetton & Joicey Colliery Co, the largest of the Durham mining companies. From its arrival in County Durham, in April 1929, it found itself very much at home, as LHJC No 52, moving the black diamonds, from inland pits, to the staithes at Sunderland.

When the coal industry was nationalised in 1947, it remained as No 52 in what became the National Coal Board's North Durham Area. It continued to work from the well-known Philadelphia depot at Houghton-le-Spring, on the Lambton Railway, until 1968. From there it was acquired for use on the KWVR where it arrived at the end of 1970.

A pleasing side view of the former Taff Vale Railway 0-6-2T in 1935, then a resident of County Durham, in the ownership of the Lambton Hetton & Joicey Colliery Co, as their No 52. Note the distinctive LHJC lettering on the side of the tank, and the cast numberplate on the bunker. The GWR-style safety-valve bonnet has been retained, while the Neilson Reid builder's plate can be discerned on the splasher above the leading driving wheel. J H L Adams collection, courtesy National Railway Museum

Right: **No 52 hauls seven wooden-bodied NCB internal user wagons, along track which hardly appears in the best of condition, at Philadelphia, County Durham, on 6th July 1967. Where once the LHJC legend stood proud in earlier days, the letters NCB can just be discerned beneath a thick layer of grime. The cast numberplate has been removed, the number 52 being stencilled on the side as well as the back of the bunker.** Peter J Fitton

No 402 *Lord Mayor*

Lord Mayor, an 0-4-0ST, is essentially a contractors locomotive, being built by established locomotive builders Hudswell Clarke & Co Ltd, Leeds, in 1893, works No 402. Tipping the scales at a mere 15½ tons, the engine was ideal for transporting from one building contract to another.

Lord Mayor enjoyed a varied career, starting out with Edmund Nuttall of Salford. It is known to have assisted in the construction of part of the Berks & Hants route, in the Castle Cary area, for the Great Western Railway, and conversely in the dismantling of the Liverpool Overhead Railway, following its closure at the end of 1956.

When its revenue earning days were over it was donated by George Cohen's of Leeds, to the Lord Mayor Trust, arriving on Worth Valley metals in June 1968. The Vintage Carriages Trust is now custodian of the engine.

When owned by George Cohen, No 402 is seen at work on the contract to dismantle the much lamented Liverpool Overhead Railway – known as 'the docker's umbrella', near Nelson Dock, on 26th October 1957. The engine has no nameplates, although the bolts used to secure these can be seen on the saddletank. J A Peden

No 752

This locomotive was originally built by Beyer Peacock, Manchester, works No 1989, for the Lancashire & Yorkshire Railway, as a class 25 0-6-0 tender engine in 1881, similar to No 52044 which we encountered earlier in the book. It carried L&Y No 752.

However, as described on page 38, following the introduction by Aspinall of a larger 0-6-0, the majority of the class 25s were rebuilt as 0-6-0STs between 1891 and 1900. No 752 was modified at Horwich Works in April 1896.

As L&Y class 23, the 230 0-6-0ST rebuilds were a common sight, in both the Red and White Rose Counties, on local goods and shunting turns. The LMS renumbered the class from 11300, No 752 becoming No 11456. BR inherited 101 of the breed in 1948, and 20 were still available for traffic in 1960. The last of the class, No 11305, a Horwich Works internal shunter,

retained its LMS number until it was withdrawn, as late as September 1964.

No 752 was allocated to Wigan (L&Y shed No 16) in 1921. It was still officially on the books of that shed as No 11456 when discarded by the LMS in April 1937. However, at the time it was on loan to the Blainscough Colliery Co Ltd, working at Welch Whittle Colliery, Coppull, who presumably were well satisfied with its performance on their 1¾ mile branch, from the pit head to the West Coast main line, for they bought the engine outright.

The number 11456 was retained, and as such it came under the control of the National Coal Board, North Western Division, Wigan Area, from January 1947. It stayed at Welch Whittle, apart from a brief spell in 1950 at Chisnall Hall Colliery, on nearby Coppull Moor, until the autumn of 1957, whereupon it was transferred to the latter on a permanent basis, except for a short sojourn on the NCB Standish system at the end of 1957.

At the end of 1958 No 11456 went to the NCB Kirkless Workshops, Wigan. It resumed duty at Ince Moss Colliery, Wigan, in April 1960, before moving to Parsonage Colliery, Leigh, in October 1961. Other than for a few weeks at the neighbouring Bickershaw Colliery from the close of 1961, it stayed at Parsonage until April 1968, when it was moved at the behest of the L&Y Saddletanks Fund to Yates Duxbury & Son Ltd, Heap Bridge Paper Mills, Heywood, for restoration. It arrived on the KWVR in November 1971.

While never a class of engine normally in the limelight, No 752 returned to Lancashire in May 1980, and took a rightful place in the Rocket 150 celebrations to commemorate the opening of the Liverpool & Manchester Railway in 1830.

No 11456 at Welch Whittle Colliery, Coppull, north of Wigan, in 1950. The wagon belongs to paper makers Cooke & Nuttall Ltd, of Horwich, and is clearly marked as 'non pool'. Frank Jones

No 1210 *Sir Berkeley*

The Manning Wardle & Co, Boyne Engine Works, Leeds, built 2,004 steam locomotives between 1859 and 1926. They concentrated on supplying small industrial and contractors engines, *Sir Berkeley* being a standard L type inside-cylindered 0-6-0ST.

As works No 1210 it was purchased new in 1891 by contractors Logan & Hemingway, and numbered 30 in their fleet. Later it became No 10. Weighing 19 tons 8½ cwt in working order, it was easily moved between building sites. It assisted on many railway construction projects, including the Great Central Railway London extension in the 1890s and, in the early 1930s, the GWR Frome and Westbury cut-off lines.

In 1935 the engine was acquired by Cranford Ironstone Co Ltd, near Kettering, who named it *Sir Berkeley*. Here, its regular daily task was to move short rakes of wagons, laden with ore from the North quarry, to the LMS exchange sidings. From 1943 to 1947 it went on loan to Pilton Quarries, near Oakham, Rutland.

During an overhaul in the mid-1950s *Sir Berkeley* received an open-back cab, in place of the original weatherboard, a welcome improvement for the crews!

In 1957 it became the reserve engine at Cranford, before being transferred to Byfield Quarries, near Banbury, in May 1959. Byfield used it for only one year before it was again relegated to stand-by duties.

Sir Berkeley was privately purchased in 1964 and, in February 1965, returned to its native Yorkshire, to the KWVR. It has since become the responsibility of the Vintage Carriages Trust.

Sir Berkeley takes a break between duties at Cranford Ironstone Quarries in 1953. Still fitted with only a basic weatherboard to protect the crew, this was rather immaterial on a warm day such as this, the driver taking the opportunity for a quick cat-nap, in what would appear to be a far from comfortable position, perched on the back of the engine! Frank Jones

Sir Berkeley stands outside the small one-road shed at Byfield Quarries on 4th October 1960. Following the fitting of a cab roof, the crew enjoy a far greater degree of protection from the elements than in earlier times although, even so, during inclement weather it was still necessary to fix a tarpaulin sheet so as to enclose the back end. Ivo Peters

No 1704 *Nunlow*

This powerful 0-6-0T, with a tractive effort of 20,800lb, was built by Hudswell Clarke & Co Ltd in 1938 as works number 1704. It had been ordered by G & T Earle Ltd, to operate a two-mile branch, connecting their cement works to the main line exchange sidings, at Hope, on the former Midland Railway Sheffield to Manchester line. It took the name *Nunlow* from the hill which once stood on the works site, the stone having been excavated for cement making in the early days and subsequently landscaped over.

During the mid-1960s, the traffic handled by *Nunlow* was taken over by diesel locomotives. After a period in storage, it was purchased by the Bahamas Locomotive Society and, in April 1969, became the first industrial engine to arrive at the new Dinting Railway Centre. Upon the closure of Dinting in 1990 *Nunlow*, along with other residents of Dinting, moved to the KWVR.

Nunlow raises steam at the Hope Cement Works of G & T Earle Ltd, in the Peak District, in 1959. Frank Jones

No 2258 *Tiny*

The Caledonia Works of Andrew Barclay Sons & Co Ltd, at Kilmarnock, constructed over 2,000 steam locomotives, the first in 1859 and the last in 1962 which was for export to Indonesia. They were one of the main suppliers to industrial users in the United Kingdom, and their locomotives could be seen throughout the country.

In 1949 Andrew Barclay supplied the North Western Gas Board with a small 0-4-0ST, works No 2258, for use at the Bradford Road Gas Works, Manchester. Here it carried the name *R. Walker*. In 1970, with no further need for the engine, the NWGB generously donated it to the Bahamas Locomotive Society. At the BLS Dinting headquarters it was appropriately renamed *Tiny*. It moved to Haworth in 1990.

Andrew Barclay No 2258 *R. Walker* is seen at Bradford Road Gas Works, Manchester, on 26th August 1967. J A Peden

No 7069

While comparatively few crane-tanks were built, they proved very useful machines, particularly at steelworks and shipyards. In Sunderland, William Doxford & Sons Ltd still had five at their Pallion shipyard in 1968.

The example on the KWVR was built by Robert Stephenson & Hawthorns, Forth Bank Works, Newcastle-upon-Tyne, in 1942, works No 7069. It pottered around Pallion yard until 1970, where it rejoiced in the name, *Southwick,* taken from a district of Sunderland.

The locomotive was purchased privately in 1971 and moved to the Dinting Railway Centre. It arrived on the KWVR in 1990 along with other former Dinting stock.

Four of the five 0-4-0CTs owned by William Doxford & Sons Ltd, can be seen in this view outside the shed in 1967. *Southwick* is prominent on the left, next to *Millfield* and *Pallion*, with either *Roker* or *Hendon* just visible in the left background. Ivo Peters

No 23 *Merlin*

Hudswell Clarke & Co Ltd, Leeds, started building internal combustion engines on a small scale during the 1920s. Over the years output gradually increased, and by the 1950s the sale of diesel locomotives had begun to outstrip that of their more traditional steam types.

In 1951 Hudswell Clarke built works No D761 for the Port of Bristol Authority, Avonmouth Docks. Basically it was one of their standard 0-6-0 diesel-mechanical designs, with a Gardner 8L3 204hp engine. The type could be modified to individual customer requirements, as was No D761, which has a larger engine compartment than normal, so as to house an auxiliary engine

It became Port of Bristol Authority No 23, and was named *Merlin*, at first working alongside steam locomotives. By 1970 steam had been eradicated from the docks, the PoBA owning a fleet of 22 diesel shunters. Thirteen had mechanical transmission, all built by Hudswell Clarke, between 1950 and 1960; the rest were Sentinels with hydraulic transmission.

With the amount of cargo shipped through the docks in decline, *Merlin* was sold in 1971 to R O Hodgson Ltd, of Carnforth, part of the English China Clays group. It then shunted their Lancashire warehouse and distribution site until 1984 when, to obviate some expensive repairs, it was replaced by former BR class 03 No 03 196.

When *Merlin* came to the KWVR in 1985, it was seen as a spares source for *Huskisson* (see opposite), but changing circumstances have made it possible to restore it to working order.

Merlin was one of a batch of four similar engines, purchased by the Port of Bristol Authority, from Hudswell Clarke between 1950 and 1955. This is No 22 *Arthur* (works No D760 built 1951), at Avonmouth Docks on 25th June 1969. *Arthur* was supplied to the PoBA in the same year as *Merlin*, and is included here since no photograph of the latter, at Bristol, has been located. Of interest is the steam type chimney – a customary feature of Hudswell Clarke diesel products in this period.
Courtesy Port of Bristol Authority

No 32 *Huskisson*

The Mersey Docks & Harbour Board tradition-ally operated a fleet of steam locomotives for shunting the docks, on both the Liverpool and Birkenhead sides of the estuary. For use in areas where there was a high fire risk from stray sparks, if conventional locomotives were used, such as near oil terminals, the Board owned a number of fireless engines.

During World War Two one of the fireless locomotives was destroyed by enemy action. In 1944, by way of replacement, the MD&HB bought a diesel-mechanical 0-6-0 from Hunslet's, works No 2699. Powered by a 204hp Gardner 8L3 engine, this was their first diesel engine, becoming No 32 in their fleet.

The locomotive spent the next 26 years on the Liverpool side of the river, shunting goods between the various docks and warehouses. However, by the start of the 1970s, declining volumes of traffic meant the MD&HB had more than enough engines for its needs and the decision was made to sell No 32.

The engine arrived on the KWVR in January 1971, having been purchased privately. It was subsequently named *Huskisson*, after the Liverpool MP, who was tragically killed, when hit by *Rocket*, on the opening day of the Liverpool & Manchester Railway, at Parkside, near Newton-le-Willows, on 15th September 1830.

Top: **This is the official Hunslet Works photograph of their No 2697, supplied to Sir Robert McAlpine & Sons in 1944. It was an identical locomotive to No 2699, sold the same year to the Mersey Docks & Harbour Board – the engine on the KWVR.**
Courtesy Hunslet Engine Co Ltd

Right: **An early photograph of No 32 at Princes Dock, Liverpool, on an unknown date.** J A Peden

Austins No 1

The Bristol-based company, Peckett & Sons Limited, will primarily be remembered for the hundreds of four and six-coupled saddletank shunting locomotives they supplied to private industry. In addition, they sold a few to the main line companies, while others were exported overseas.

In the late 1950s, with the demand for their steam products declining, Peckett's attempted to develop their business by entering the grow-ing diesel market. In the event they produced only five. The last was works No 5003, a diesel-mechanical 0-4-0, utilising a Gardner 8L3 204hp engine. It left Bristol in 1961, after standing idle for three years awaiting a buyer, destined for James Austin & Son (Dewsbury) Ltd.

For the next three years, as Austins No 1, the engine was kept busy shunting their West Riding iron and steel stockholding site, and transferring wagons to and from the BR inter-change sidings. After this, with Austin's connec-tion to BR severed, it found occasional use on works internal traffic until 1971.

With no further need of the engine at Dewsbury, Austin's then unselfishly made it available to the KWVR on permanent loan, a valuable addition to the line's diesel shunting stock.

Austins No 1 at James Austin & Son (Dewsbury) Ltd, iron and steel stockholding site, in the 1960s. Sydney A Leleux

James

James, a small four-wheeled diesel-electric locomotive, capable of generating 165hp, was built by Ruston & Hornsby Ltd, of Lincoln, in 1959, works No 431763. It was purchased by Stewarts & Lloyds Ltd, for use at their Bilston Iron and Steel Works, near Wolverhampton.

During the 1970s the Bilston plant, then owned by the British Steel Corporation, operated a fleet of 15 0-4-0DEs, two from Ruston & Hornsby, the remainder built by the Yorkshire Engine Company Ltd. However, towards the end of the decade a reduction in rail traffic meant a number of the locomotives could be taken out of service, James being among them.

The engine was then bought by Tilsley & Lovatt Ltd, a company which renovated and traded in diesel locomotives. It was moved during the summer of 1980 to their Trentham Works, near Stoke-on-Trent, and given a complete overhaul. Unfortunately, with industry having less and less of a need for railway locomotives, no buyer was forthcoming.

James remained at Trentham until 1987 when, through a private purchase, it was secured for the Dinting Railway Centre. This camera-shy locomotive moved to the KWVR when the Dinting project folded in 1990.

No photograph of James in its pre-preservation days has come to hand. It is very similar to the locomotive illustrated here, Ruston & Hornsby No 434774 built 1961, a fellow member of the RH 165DE class, seen at the Yorkshire Water Authority, Blackburn Meadows Sewage Works, Sheffield, on 16th April 1983. In all RH constructed 164 165DEs, 21 of which had an 0-6-0 wheel arrangement, weighing 30 tons, unlike James and the rest with four-wheels, which registered 28 tons on the scales.
J A Peden

No 118 *Brussels*

In addition to the former BR locomotives Nos 30072 and 68077, there are another three ex-Army engines on the KWVR whose origins go back to the Second World War. The first of these, *Brussels*, an 'Austerity' 0-6-0ST (see No 68077 page 43) was Hunslet-designed but constructed by their Leeds neighbours, Hudswell Clarke in 1945, as works No 1782. When new it was delivered to the Longmoor Military Railway, Liss, Hampshire, the army training railway.

Following the end of World War Two, the War Department decided to keep 90 'Austerities' for shunting and operating their own establishments, as well as for future training purposes. In 1947 they were numbered 100 to 189, *Brussels* becoming No 118. A further 14 'Austerities' were purchased new in 1953 from Hunslet.

The locomotive was named *Brussels* in 1950. Unfortunately it suffered an accident in June 1953, whereupon it lay derelict for some five years, before, in 1958, it was decided to send the engine to Hunslet's for attention. During the overhaul *Brussels* was converted to oil-firing, and had Westinghouse air-brakes and electric-lighting fitted. Back at Longmoor, army personnel continued to be trained on the locomotive until 1966, thereafter it fell out of use.

The authorities decided to close Longmoor in 1970, and while there were some ambitious plans for the site as a preservation centre and some ex-BR engines had already been assembled there, these came to naught. The collapse of the scheme meant new homes had to be found for the locomotives, including *Brussels*, which a short time previously had been purchased privately. The engine was bought by the KWVR in September 1971. Since then some beneficial modifications have been carried out to the oil burning equipment.

A close-up view of *Brussels* at Longmoor, on 16th April 1966. Part of the saddletank has been cut away to accommodate the Westinghouse air-braking system, and an electric headlamp is mounted above the smokebox door. Gavin Morrison

No 1931

During World War Two there was a dire need for additional heavy freight locomotives, both to assist on the home-front, and to be readily available for shipment to Europe, in the wake of the anticipated opening of the second front by the Allied forces. The War Department's brief was for a simple, robust machine, yet one that would be reliable under the most adverse of circumstances.

The very austere looking WD 2-8-0s, built under the direction of R A Riddles, proved admirable for the purpose. Such was the demand that between 1943 and 1945 frames were laid for 935 examples, 545 by the North British Locomotive Company in Glasgow, and 390 at Vulcan Foundry, Newton-le-Willows. All but three saw service in Europe.

A heavier 2-10-0 version at 78 tons 6 cwt was also constructed, these having a wider route availability than the 2-8-0s, due to their lighter

Once peace had been restored, the need for their services in Europe was much reduced. Before long, many were on their way back to Britain across the North Sea or the English Channel. Some were soon in use again on home soil, the LNER purchasing 200 outright, and classifying them as 07s. After nationalisation BR added a further 533 to its stock. They were numbered 90000 to 90732 and ranged far and wide over the system.

A sizable number of WD engines were destined never to return to their homeland, and both the 2-8-0 and 2-10-0 classes played a significant role in the rejuvenation of the Netherlands Railways, which were in a very bad state at the end of the war. In December 1945 the NSR had 227 of these 2-8-0s available for traffic, 184 staying on a permanent basis. They were diagrammed for passenger as well as freight services.

It was one of these NSR locomotives, Vulcan Foundry built No 5200, new in January 1945, WD No 79257, that eventually found its way to the Worth Valley, albeit by a very circuitous

route. As NSR No 4464 from August 1945, in line with the other WDs that stayed in Holland, it received various modifications, the most obvious being a chimney extension. Steam heating was fitted for use on passenger services. In Holland they were commonly referred to as 'Dakotas'.

Records of the engine in Holland are sketchy, but it is known to have been attached to Rietlanden shed at the beginning of 1949, together with 11 of her sisters. In August 1950 it was one of 10 shedded at Eindhoven.

Barely two years old, the future KWVR ex-WD 2-8-0 is pictured in Holland in 1947, as NS No 4464. A detailed look at the photograph reveals only a few differences to the 733 that worked for BR, the most noticeable being the extended chimney, a ladder above the leading driving wheel, air-braking equipment, and the headlights above the buffers. J P Rond

Below: **On 28th September 1972 No 1931 looks none the worse for its 14 years in storage, in the arctic conditions, which prevail for much of the year, at Mellansjo, Sweden. The photograph was taken while the engine was under inspection, prior to its return to England.** Richard S Greenwood

Opposite page: **Just as the WDs are remembered by the majority of British enthusiasts, No 90625, then allocated to Wakefield (56A), clanks slowly past Leeds, Holbeck shed with a seemingly never-ending rake of empty coal wagons, on 23rd August 1966. Ten months later No 90625 was withdrawn and subsequently scrapped, the fate suffered by all 733 WD 2-8-0s once on the books of BR. When next No 1931 turns a wheel it will look as No 90625 does in this picture and be numbered 90733.** Tom Heavyside

uring the 1950s, electrification of the rail-
 in Holland proceeded apace, and with the
n from Germany of some of their own loco-
tives, the WD fleet was gradually withdrawn.
ile the last of the NSR 2-10-0s was sent for
rap in 1951, a few of their smaller 2-8-0 coun-
rparts fared much better, some soldiering on
o 1958, when Holland became the first coun-
 in Europe to dispense with steam on its
ational network, ten years before BR.
   Meanwhile, in June 1953, two of the class
ere made available to the Swedish State
ailways, Nos 4464 and 4383 (NB No 25428 of
944). They first went to Orebro Works where
ey had fully enclosed cabs fitted, necessary to
elp the crew combat the very severe winter
emperatures experienced in that country, electric lighting and a steam turbo-generator, along

with other standard Swedish fittings. The tender
was shortened, the original four axles being
reduced to three, since otherwise the ensemble
would have been too long to fit on Swedish
turntables.

As Swedish Railways class G11 Nos 1930
(NS No 4383) and 1931 (NS No 4464), they
worked between Nassjo and Halmstad, in the
south of the country. In 1958 it was decided the
G11s should be mothballed, as part of the SJ
strategic reserve stock. They were moved to a
remote forest clearing at Mellansjo for storage.

There they languished, until 1972, when
some intrepid travellers from the Worth Valley
motored to Sweden and arranged for the repa-
triation of No 1931. It arrived in West Yorkshire
during January 1973, being brought to Haworth
on a low-loader from Hull docks.

Before the engine could be used on home
soil, it was necessary to lower the cab roof and
remove the chimney extension, so as to comply
with the British loading gauge. As such it was
more readily identifiable as a former WD-owned
locomotive.

No 1931 has been out of action for some
years, and it is intended to return it to service in
the guise of a former BR-owned WD, as No
90733. This would have been the next available
number in the BR series. With no former BR WD
2-8-0s preserved, despite some working into
1967, it will be especially welcomed in this form,
filling a significant gap in the ranks of Britain's
preserved locomotives. A number of the larger
WD 2-10-0s are still extant.

No 5820

No 5820 is representative of another class of engine whose genesis came about due to the urgent need for more freight engines during World War Two. Built for the United States Army Transportation Corps the class S160s were typically American in outline, having bar frames, a high-pitched boiler, and much external pipework, all of this within the British loading gauge.

Between 1942 and 1945 it is understood a staggering 2120 were put together. The work was shared fairly evenly between the American Locomotive Company, Baldwin Locomotive Works and Lima Locomotive Works. All but a handful were shipped across the Atlantic as deck cargo, the first arrivals being landed at British west coast ports in the autumn of 1942.

Of the early imports 400 were deputed to assist the then somewhat beleaguered British railway companies, while a similar number were dumped in South Wales, pending the day they could be moved to mainland Europe.

From late 1944 the S160s started to be shipped to the Continent. The first to go were the stored engines, before those assisting the 'Big Four' were commandeered by the Authorities, while some later built S160s went direct to Europe. It is believed 18 lie at the bottom of the oceans due to enemy action.

USATC No 5820 was manufactured by Lima Locomotive Works, Ohio, in 1945, works No 8758. It was shipped to Britain, although within a month was moved on to France.

Once peace had been restored in 1945, the S160s became widely scattered throughout Europe, and indeed elsewhere. Many countries, particularly some in what became part of the Eastern bloc, eagerly accepted them as a quick way of supplementing their own depleted motive power resources. Some moved on to China and South Korea, while others, built to 5ft 6in gauge, went to India. Only one returned to Britain, in August 1946, WD No 700, which remained at Longmoor until scrapped in 1957.

After the war Polish Railways were glad to get their hands on some 500 S160s, mainly for freight work. By 1969 only 32 had been withdrawn. A survivor was No Tr203.474 (USATC No 5820), believed to have spent the majority of its time allocated to Katowice shed. At some time

or other it received the boiler from an Alco engine, which it still carries.

During the 1970s steam in Poland wa decline. Simultaneously the British preservat movement, including men from the West Ridir were casting the net far and wide in a search additional motive power.

In 1977 attention turned to No 5820, desp the obvious difficulties in arranging its mov ment to England.

The engine arrived at Haworth in Novemb 1977, and soon became popularly known a 'Big Jim'. The following summer it reverted to USATC identity as No 5820 and took part making the feature film 'Yanks'.

While the class are definitely not the enthus asts favourite, the S160s certainly have a rightfu place in Britain's railway history. They also played a much valued part, alongside the British WD 'Austerity' classes, in bringing about a successful conclusion to World War Two, and later in assisting the rebuilding operations. Since 'Big Jim's' arrival another four have been imported from Europe, along with one from China, whilst other examples of the type have been retained in various parts of the world.

Left: **Tr203.474 (the former USATC No 5820) on the right, in company with a sister class S160, pose by the turntable, in front of the shed building at Katowice shed, Poland, in the mid-1970s.** Robin Higgins

Below: **Illustrative of some of the work undertaken by the S160s in Poland is this photograph of No Tr203.228 shunting at Sierpc in July 1976.** Peter J C Skelton